LEGENDARY HORROR FILMS

LEGENDARY HORROR FILMS

- **Essential genre history** • **Offscreen anecdotes**
- **Special effects secrets** • **Ghoulish facts and photographs**

Peter Guttmacher

MetroBooks

MetroBooks

An Imprint of Friedman/Fairfax Publishers

Library of Congress Cataloging-in-Publication Data
Guttmacher, Peter.
    Legendary horror: essential genre history, offscreen anecdotes,
special effects secrets, ghoulish facts and photographs / Peter
Guttmacher.
        p.   cm.
    Includes bibliographical references and index.
    ISBN 1-56799-171-8
    1. Horror films—History and criticism.   I. Title.
PN1995.9.H6G88   1995
791.43'616—dc20   95-13529
                                                               CIP

Editor: Elizabeth Viscott Sullivan
Art Director: Jeff Batzli
Designer: Lynne Yeamans
Photography Editor: Wendy Missan

Color separations by Ocean Graphic International Company Ltd.
Printed in China by Leefung-Asco Printers Ltd.

For bulk purchases and special sales, please contact:
Friedman/Fairfax Publishers
Attention: Sales Department
15 West 26th Street
New York, NY 10010
212/685-6610   FAX 212/685-1307

ACKNOWLEDGMENTS

The author wishes to thank the following institutions for providing horrifying information: The Louis B. Mayer Library at the American Film Institute, the Margaret Herrick Research Library at the Academy of Motion Picture Arts and Sciences, the Los Angeles County Library in West Hollywood, the Beverly Hills Library, and the main branch of the Santa Monica Public Library. He'd also like to thank Robin Brownstein, Matthew Hoffman, Elizabeth Sullivan, Maryanne Melloan, and Scott Lundius for unnerving guidance.

CONTENTS

INTRODUCTION

There is no escaping the fear now. Alone in the dark, you sit unblinking, white-knuckled with dread. Your hands are moist, ready to shield your eyes from what they will be forced to witness. You tensely peer into the blackness, your heart hammering, your stomach winding into an ever-tightening knot. As you sense the imminent terror, your knees involuntarily creep up to your chest. Every muscle poised for fight or flight, breath held in limbo, throat clenched to stifle the rising scream within it, you finally lose all control. Your brain shrieks, "For God's sake, don't go in there!"

Then Tippi Hedren opens the attic door to look for birds. Then a kid gets cozy for a nap on Elm Street. Then the sun sets just as Professor Van Helsing is walking into Dracula's crypt. Then Sigourney Weaver decides to get sentimental and look for her cat on the spaceship *Nostromo*. Then Janet Leigh decides to freshen up with a quick shower at the Bates Motel. Then the tourists plunge back into the water along the beaches of Amity, Long Island,....*Then bad things happen.*

When the lights come back up, you're a wreck. Your pulse is still beating like crazy, your eyes are dilated, geese are still paddling across your back, your stomach feels like it's inhabited by an epileptic octopus, and tonight you'll probably have nightmares. Oh yes...but next weekend you'll pay good money to go through it all over again.

⁂

Horror films have been a passion verging on addiction for movie audiences almost as long as images have been flickering across the silver screen. And why not? What other popular escape provides in-depth examinations of good and evil (*Dr. Jekyll and Mr. Hyde*), metaphysical questioning (*Jacob's Ladder*), environmental and technological warnings (*It Came from Beneath the Sea* and *The Stand*), the mythic retelling of primeval fights for survival

OPPOSITE: Saints "preserve" us! Down in the dark front cellar, Lila Crane (Vera Miles) makes the acquaintance of Norman Bates' maniacal mother in Alfred Hitchcock's classic Psycho (1960).

(*Alien*), or a mirror held to manage the tabloid monsters of real life (*The Silence of the Lambs*)?

Horror has carved a strange, circular path to the present through the past century or two. Gothic tales of terror and the macabre from the 1800s fed the visionary imaginations of German expressionist filmmakers in the early twentieth century, and they in turn breathed new life into a budding American film industry in the early twenties, which created a golden age of horror classics in the thirties, which spun off to both brilliant and embarrassing low-budget films in the forties that were mutated by the scientific horrors inspired by World War II and its aftermath of political paranoia in the fifties, which reconnected with horror's roots in the late sixties and early seventies, which spurred counterculture filmmakers to explore uncharted psychological and spiritual territory and which made horror fiction so popular in the seventies and eighties, which has once again been translated back to the screen for horror's Oscar-winning resurgence in the eighties and nineties! What goes around comes around.

From silents to special effects megahits, Hollywood horror has made an amazing journey. Consider this book your insider's tour of its hideous high points as well as a few of its more infamous lows. Settle down in a safe place. Prepare to explore blockbusters, beautiful B pictures, cult classics, and the little-known gems of the genre. Get ready to go behind the scenes to learn production secrets. Meet the horror makers and stars whose lives were sometimes as unsettling as their films. Brace yourself for disturbing parallels between real life and the most terrifying movies ever made. Sharpen your H.Q. (Horror Quotient) with truly horrible trivia and knowledge tests. And of course, learn what's in Room 101.

As Richard Burton patiently explained while leading John Hurt down that long dark hallway in *1984* (1984), "You know what's in Room 101, Winston. Everyone knows what's in Room 101....The thing that is in Room 101 is the worst thing in the world. It goes beyond fear of pain or of death. It is unendurable. And it varies from individual to individual. It may be burial alive, or castration, or...many other things. In your case it's rats." What is *it* in your case? Just step inside and find out.

Chapter One

OLD MASTERS OF MAYHEM, THE MACABRE, AND MONSTROSITY

The aftermath of the plagues that ravaged late-medieval Europe brought a boom of artistic ghastliness, especially sculpture, that seems to prefigure the worst of twentieth-century horror. All the icons are there: grinning skulls, beckoning skeletons, putrid tableaux that virtually reek. Yet these images were both realistic (because those who saw them had very likely seen the real things) and monitory (because they meant to chasten the observer, to remind him of life's brevity and urge him toward salvation).

—Walter Kendrick, The Thrill of Fear, 1991

The face that launched a thousand shrieks: Lon Chaney unmasked in The Phantom of the Opera *(1925), revealing the most memorable makeup in horror history.*

WRITTEN IN BLOOD

There have always been horrible things to write about. The Bible immortalized giants. The ancient Greeks had the horrors of war and political upheaval. The plays of Sophocles, Euripides, and their peers included gruesome doings, such as a mother feeding a pie stuffed with children to her husband, or an incestuous son gouging his eyes out for what he did to mommy and daddy.

Medieval times fed horrific holy food to the minds of its authors. Beowulf righteously slaughtered Grendel, the monster. Stories celebrating the lives of the saints depicted in lurid detail the tortures of both the damned and living Christians. Pestilence slaughtered twenty-five million Europeans within a five-year period in the fourteenth century. Fifteenth-century Wallachian warlord Vlad Tepes became one of the most monumental sadists of all time, ascending from man into myth as Dracula, the blood drinker. Even the fairy tales from the Brothers Grimm and other children's writers contained macabre lessons. Bluebeard was a wife murderer. Hansel and Gretel were at the mercy of a cannibalistic witch. Little Red Riding Hood got to cuddle up to the world's first wolf masquerading as a human.

The prototypical Gothic horror novel, or horror for the fun of it, came shortly after the first of these novels was penned. Rumor has it that the book was the result of a nightmare visited upon Horace Walpole, a peculiar Englishman who had built a medieval castle on his estate in the mid-1700s. Walpole's book, *The Castle of Otranto* (1764), was set in—you guessed it—a castle and reveled in familial madness and murder.

Stealthily, a new literary appetite wormed its way into the repressed, seething Victorian mind. Gothic horror novels and stories were soon very popular, and among them towered the giant works that later inspired the first horror filmmakers. By 1816, Prussia's E. T. A. Hoffman had delivered his chilling bedtime story of evil and automatons, *The Sandman*. Two years later, Mary Shelley wrote *Frankenstein* on a bet. American master Edgar Allan Poe was in his delirious prime by the mid-1840s, and short stories were "nevermore" the same. *Treasure Island*'s beloved author,

Robert Louis Stevenson, penned *The Strange Case of Dr. Jekyll and Mr. Hyde* in 1888. H. G. Wells wrote his animal-rights nightmare, *The Island of Doctor Moreau*, in 1896, and Bram Stoker gave the world a taste for blood with a fictional *Dracula* in 1897.

UNHALLOWED GROUNDBREAKERS

Early Film Experiments in Silent Horror

Somehow, it's fitting that a magician should have made the first horror films. During film's infancy, Georges Méliès attended the historic 1895 Paris Universelle (World's Fair) exhibition. There, upon viewing the Lumière brothers' cinematography exhibit, he had a brilliant idea, one that would change celluloid history. Méliès decided to use film to create the illusion of the fantastic.

By May 1897, Méliès had constructed his own film studio at Montreuil. He must have been busy, because by the turn of the century he had shot 244 short films, including *The Devil's Castle* (the first vampire movie), *The Haunted Castle* (the first ghost movie), and his legendary interpretation of fellow Frenchman Jules Verne's space adventure, *A Trip to the Moon* (the first movie with a monster in it). Other Méliès flights of fancy included *The Man with Four Heads*, *The Laboratory of Mephistopheles*, *The Merry Frolics of Satan*, and *The Conquest of the Pole* (in which the Abominable Snowman appeared for the first time).

Though his studio was bankrupt by 1913, leaving him peddling candy and toys from a Paris kiosk five years later, Méliès' films had made it to the United States in 1903, where they did not go unnoticed. Pioneering American director Edwin S. Porter swiftly borrowed from Méliès' style of screen illusions for his nightmare *Dreams of a Rarebit Friend* (1906).

A young American film industry slowly got into the horror swing. Producer William N. Selig brought Mr. Hyde and his better half to the screen in 1908. D. W. Griffith released a film of Ferenc Molnar's popular play *The Devil* in 1909 and adapted Poe's "The Tell-Tale Heart" to *The Avenging Conscience* in 1914. The father of motion pictures, Thomas Alva Edison, delivered a one-reel rendering of *Frankenstein* in 1910.

Still, Europe continued to be more fertile ground for horror films. Abel Gance, later of *Napoleon* fame, directed the distortion-filled *The Madness of Dr. Tube* in 1915. In Germany, where the artistic avant-garde was flowering, the Deutsche Bioscop company released several wonderfully macabre works produced by, starring, and often adapted by the actor Paul Wegener.

Wegener's *Der Student von Prag* ("The Student of Prague," 1913) was horror's first feature. At seventy-five minutes, the film

No Santa Claus here: the fertile mind of early filmmaker Georges Méliès made even the Arctic a fearsome place in The Conquest of the Pole (1912).

was a variation of doppelgänger themes found in Poe's story "William Wilson" and in Hoffman's story "The Doubles." In this film, the hero makes a Faustian deal, selling his literal mirror image to a wizard for fame and fortune. When the bargain sours and the demented young man murders the wizard to regain his reflection, he accidentally cracks the mirror image, thus tearing apart his body and soul.

Wegener's *Der Golem, wie er in die Welt kam* ("The Golem and How He Came into the World," 1914), the real grandfather of all monster movies, plays upon a Jewish legend of a sixteenth-century Prague rabbi who built a creature from clay to protect his people from a pogrom. But in the film version, the creature runs amok and has to be deactivated. The man-made–monster theme was a winner, and the abstract expressionistic set design as well as Karl Freund's creepily fluid camera style would become staples of the American genre.

Two of the most influential horror silents out of Germany were produced in the early twenties. It seems that screenwriter Carl

RIGHT: Paul Wegener contemplates the wages of sin after having sold his soul in The Student of Prague *(1913). BELOW: The party's over when Der Golem brings down the roof in the 1920 film that bore his name.*

Mayer had had unpleasant experiences with psychologists while serving in the army. Mayer's partner, Hans Janowitz, was convinced that he had spotted a man who he believed to be a notorious sex murderer in Hamburg masquerading as a bourgeois

gentleman in 1913. Director Robert Wiene's father had gone insane. Together, their three wounded psyches fashioned a film about sanatoriums, somnambulists, and things being much more sinister than they seem.

Das Kabinett von Dr. Caligari ("The Cabinet of Dr. Caligari," 1919) was horror's first international hit. In it German horror star Conrad Veidt (he later played Humphrey Bogart's Nazi nemesis in *Casablanca*) plays a gaunt fortune-telling sleepwalker kept in a coffin by a sideshow hypnotist in the little town of Holstenwall.

Strange stabbing murders plague the town's populace, and it soon becomes apparent, at least to one young man, that the hypnotist has been sending his sleepwalker on errands of evil. Veidt, slink-sliding his way down alleyways at night, is a sight to behold. The crazily angled sets, courtesy of the avant-garde Strum Group, took expressionism to its limits. The plot twist at the end still fools even jaded horror fans.

Friedrich Wilhelm Murnau had directed Veidt as both Satan and Jekyll (and Hyde) in 1919 and 1920 films, but he didn't hit the big time until he made his masterpiece, *Nosferatu* ("The Undead," 1922). Loosely based on Stoker's *Dracula*—so loosely, in fact, that Murnau hadn't bothered to get permission from Stoker's estate and was eventually sued by his widow, and most copies of the film were destroyed—it starred Max Schreck (there's a name for a horror star) as Count Orlock, the scuttling, talon-nailed, bald-headed, bat-eared, rat-toothed bloodsucker who, unlike Stoker's prototype, could be destroyed by the sun's rays.

The rest is vampire history.

HORROR HAS ITS USES

The great American actor John Barrymore made his uncanny transformation from good to evil in the 1920 silent film Dr. Jekyll and Mr. Hyde without the benefit of any cosmetic help. But in later scenes where Hyde was at his grotesque best, Barrymore used makeup, fangs, talonlike nails, and a lanky, greasy wig. Barrymore dusted off these tools seven years later when he went house buying.

Going to offer a price on King Vidor's $60,000 mansion, Barrymore waited, a hideous apparition behind the window of his limousine, while his manager anonymously negotiated with the famous director for his digs. Barrymore grimaced, twitched, and cackled behind the glass, even going so far as to kiss and fondle the pet monkey he had brought along with him. Vidor was so unnerved by this mysterious buyer that he dropped his price down to $50,000. (Think how much lower he'd have gone if Barrymore had only added blood pellets.)

John Barrymore (right) was never more at home than when he played this savage seducer in the silent version of Robert Louis Stevenson's Dr. Jekyll and Mr. Hyde (1920).

Don't Step on That Spider. It Might Be Lon Chaney!

If there was ever a horror star's horror star, an actor's actor, and a tragic hero rolled into one, it was "The Man of a Thousand Faces," a.k.a. Alonso Chaney. Although he starred in only eight films that were technically in the horror genre, most of his fifty other roles were so macabre—Chaney almost unrecognizably transformed himself in many of them—that he became a horror legend and one of Universal Studio's highest-paid stars.

Chaney was born in Colorado Springs, Colorado, on April 1, 1883. His parents were deaf-mutes, yet his mother was in charge of putting on the local school's pantomimes and pageants, and had her son onstage by the time he was three. Chaney himself refused to utter a single word—on- or offstage—until he was eight years old, preferring instead to communicate as his parents did, through pantomime and sign language. By the age of ten, Chaney had quit school to care for his mother, who had become hideously crippled by inflammatory arthritis. This disease was to be the beginning of his long, strange relationship with physical pain and deformity.

Chaney had sharpened his acting teeth (something he later appeared to have actually done for his vampire role in the 1927 film *London After Midnight*) with years of work in touring theater and vaudeville acts. A former prop man, decorator, drapery worker, and wardrobe master, he knew the importance of appearance on stage as well as how to achieve a wealth of illusory effects with makeup and costume.

In 1905, he married a fifteen-year-old singer, Cleva Creighton, after only three days' acquaintance. The following year, the couple had a son, Creighton Chaney (a.k.a. Lon Chaney, Jr., a.k.a. "The Wolf Man"). Tired of making $12 a week on the road and of performing at small-town saloons while his boy pocketed food from the free-lunch counter, Chaney moved his wife and son to Los Angeles shortly before 1910. But Cleva was a much more popular stage commodity than he, and he deeply resented her for it. It didn't take long before he was pressuring her to stay at home with their son and accusing her of infidelity. Cleva took to drink and, at the height of their marital troubles, swallowed poison at a theater where Chaney was performing, effectively destroying her vocal cords as a result. Chaney had her institutionalized and divorced her, then told his young son that his mother had died. By 1915, Chaney had fallen in love with a chorus girl named Hazel Hastings, who soon divorced her legless husband to marry the stage actor.

Shortly after he remarried, Chaney left the stage to try his luck as a film actor at Universal Studios. With his experience, aptitude for character work, and makeup kit in hand, Chaney soon made himself indispensable, able to play almost every part imaginable. As his son remembered, "He used to sit in the bullpen at Universal,

Is he a bat or is he just bats? Only Lon Chaney could have so much fun being so scary in the tragically lost vampire thriller London After Midnight (1927).

which was a room about the size of this TV studio. He'd sit there and an assistant director would come out and say, 'Anybody here that can play a college boy?' Dad would say, 'Yeah, I can play a college boy.' Then he'd come back and they'd come out and say, 'Anybody play a Chinaman?'...he'd say, 'Yeah, I can play a Chinaman.' He'd make himself up as a Chinaman, go work for ten minutes, come back, then go out and play a Greek. And this way make three or four pictures a day."

By 1918, at the age of thirty-five, the versatile actor was a valued bit player on the Universal lot, although he was still only making $5 a day. When he asked the studio manager for a raise to $125 a week with a five-year contract, he was turned down flat. Chaney then walked out, even though times were bad. At first, leaving seemed like a foolish move, but employment finally and ironically came from western star William S. Hart, who had admired Chaney's work. Hart asked him to costar with a sizable villain's role in the horse opera *Riddle Gawne*.

This film garnered Chaney the attention he deserved, soon bringing him a gamut of juicy character roles, including gangsters, pirates, beggars, comics, and cripples. The last category is where Chaney's real break came and where his true genius lay. In 1919, director George Loane Tucker was casting *The Miracle Man*. The star role was that of Frog, a cripple who is saved by faith healing. A contortionist had been tested for the role but couldn't act. Chaney was given a chance, and while preparing for the screen test, he discovered a trick. He later recalled, "While I was sitting pondering over the part I unconsciously did a trick I've done since childhood. I crossed my legs, then double-crossed them, wrapping my left foot around my right ankle. When I came to the studio on the test day, Tucker was already behind the camera. He gave me one glance and called, "Camera!" I flopped down, dragging myself forward along the floor, my eyes rolling, my face twitching and my legs wrapped tighter and tighter around each other. Tucker didn't speak

and the sweat rolled off me. Finally I heard a single whispered word from him. 'God,' Tucker said. I wanted to say that too, but not for the same reason."

Suffering aside, *The Miracle Man* was a hit. In his next film, *The Penalty* (1920), Chaney starred as a legless criminal genius. Preparation for this role was even more masochistic, thanks to leg binding in an excruciating leather harness, but a pay increase to $500 a week eased his pain.

Pain, pathos, deformity, and diversity soon became Chaney's specialties. Chameleonlike, he often played two characters in the same film. Armless knife throwers, dead-legged magicians, half-blind gangsters, crippled bishops, mistreated clowns, diabolical ventriloquists in drag—the stranger the role, the more zealously and painfully he worked to get under his character's skin, and almost always did so with unnerving success. Chaney had some memorable mainstream roles, but on the whole, he preferred to play freaks and went to greater and greater lengths to disfigure himself for these parts.

Chaney's first official horror film came in 1922 with *A Blind Bargain*, in which he played both an apeman and the mad scientist who had de-evolved him by surgically fitting him with monkey glands. But it was the following year that Chaney landed the role that would thrust horror into the mainstream, make him Universal's number one box-office draw, and boost his salary to over $10,000 a month.

The Hunchback of Notre Dame (1923), based on the Victor Hugo classic, placed Chaney in the spotlight as Quasimodo, the misshapen beastlike bell ringer whose love for Esmeralda, a persecuted gypsy girl, leads him to take on what seems like the whole population of Paris. The film set took more than a year to build on Universal's back lot, where the edifice of the great cathedral stands to this day. The film itself took four months to shoot, with an

OPPOSITE: The undisputed king of communicating human (and in this case, simian) suffering, Chaney reaches out to his maker in A Blind Bargain (1922). TOP: "The Man of a Thousand Faces" faces down an intruder in The Miracle Man (1919). ABOVE: The atmosphere is pure fear and loathing in this scene from The Penalty (1920), for which Chaney designed his own instrument of self-torture.

army of over five hundred extras. For Chaney, it meant a grueling four and a half hours of daily makeup preparation, for he followed Hugo's description of Quasimodo to the very letter.

The film was shot in the summer, and the physical pain and intense heat Chaney endured in his costume, makeup, and hump harness were mammoth. During the filming, Chaney's father began to lose his sight. In despair over his already disabled father's misfortune, the five-foot-five-inch (162.5cm) actor hurled himself into his work, soon sought out the gigantic Mexican actor Nick De Ruiz, and requested that he let out all the stops in the scene where he was to bullwhip Chaney's character.

However twisted its root, the suffering paid off. A review in *Bioscope* magazine proclaimed: "His [Chaney's] extraordinary make-up as a veritable living gargoyle reaches the limit of grotesquery (and at moments seems to go a shade beyond it) but his sprawling movements and frantic gestures are brilliantly conceived, and his final dance of frenzy at the defeat of Clopin's rabble is a scene of delirious passion which has seldom been equalled on the screen."

The humanity Chaney brought to Quasimodo's monstrosity made the film one of the year's most popular. But the torment he put his body and mind through landed him a three-month hospital stint after the cameras stopped rolling.

Two years later, Chaney performed his towering horror achievement as the hideously deformed Eric in *The Phantom of the Opera* (1925). Based on the Gaston LeRoux novel, the film featured Chaney as the mad masked organist who terrorizes the Paris Opera House and lures an operatic beauty down to his mausoleumlike home far beneath the city's streets and sewers. The scene where his captive flower tears off his mask, revealing a living skull, shows the most unforgettable face in horror history. There were no special effects and no latex, just the brilliance of "The Man of a Thousand Faces" and his makeup kit.

Reporters often suggested that Chaney's extensive transformation efforts were masochistic. Chaney, however, was guarded about his techniques, saying only that "there are tricks in my peculiar trade that I don't care to divulge any more than a magician will give away his art," although he did admit that his work as a tour-

ing stage manager gave him a great familiarity with the tricks that light can play on an actor's face.

Chaney's stage work held him in good stead in other ways, too. Unlike many silent stars, Chaney survived the terrifying shift into the talkies. He frankly admitted in a 1930 interview that "my first talking picture is going to make me or break me." So to make the break, he studied sound equipment with the same zealous perfectionism that he brought to acting. His debut was a 1930 remake of his macabre silent hit *The Unholy Three* (1925), which teamed him up with a strong man and a midget. During the film, Chaney served up the voices of a ventriloquist, his dummy, an old woman, a girl, and a parrot.

The reviews of the film practically deified Chaney. One critic went so far as to predict that "the industry will never be the same again." Tragically, neither would Chaney. The years of contorting himself had damaged his spine. Makeup to replicate blindness had damaged his vision. His throat had long bothered him since it had been irritated by a piece of synthetic snow while filming a railroad picture in 1929. Shortly after filming *The Unholy Three*, he was diagnosed with bronchial cancer. Ironically, with his voice gone in his last days, the master of the macabre had to revert to the pantomime and sign language he had clung to for the first eight years of his life. He died on August 26, 1930 at forty-seven.

Wonder-boy producer Irving Thalberg best assessed Chaney's greatness in the eulogy he gave at the actor's crowded funeral service. He dubbed Chaney great "not only because of his God-given talent but because he used that talent to illuminate certain dark corners of the human spirit. He showed the world the souls of those people who were born different from the rest."

ABOVE: This lobby card tempted many into viewing **The Phantom of the Opera** *(1925). LEFT: The master of this motley crew, Chaney calls the shots in perhaps his finest film achievement,* **The Unholy Three** *(1925). OPPOSITE: As the demented organist, Chaney takes a break from practice to terrorize his captive flower, played by Mary Philbin, in* **The Phantom of the Opera.**

GENIUS IS PAIN,
OR IT'S THE HUMP THAT HURTS!

Chaney did not reveal many of his makeup techniques, but for the nonsqueamish, here are a few of the surviving secrets that helped further his magical and masochistic changes.

THE PENALTY *(1920): To appear amputated, Chaney designed a leather harness to bind his calves to his thighs, wrapped them with leather, and added leather nubs at the bottom. This caused him excruciating pain in scenes where he jumped down onto his stumps.*

THE HUNCHBACK OF NOTRE DAME *(1923): Chaney wore a 72-pound (32.4kg) rubber hump attached to a harness that was attached to a breastplate, making it impossible to stand erect. He totally*

occluded one eye, wore a rubber bodysuit matted with animal hair during summer shooting, and inserted a device that made his mouth always hang open.

THE PHANTOM OF THE OPERA *(1925): Chaney inserted a device that drastically spread his nostrils and turned up his nose, giving his proboscis the look of a skull's snout. He jammed celluloid disks into his cheeks to distort his cheekbones, and attached false teeth with prongs to draw back the corners of his lips in a death's-head grimace.*

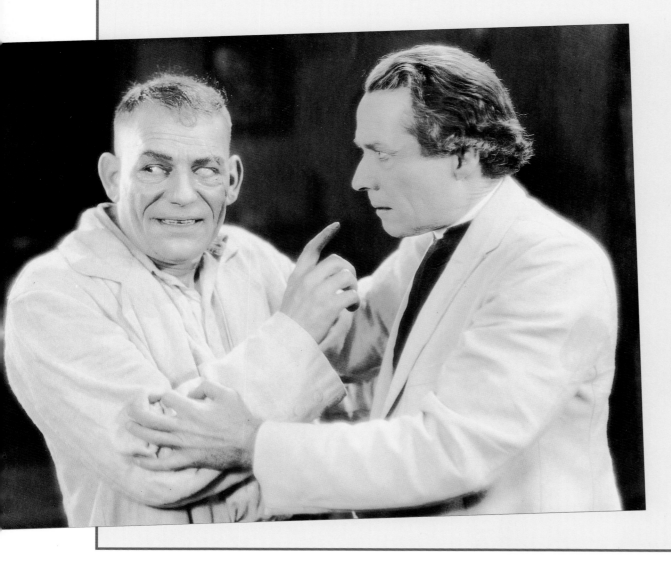

LEFT: Believe it or not, the one-eyed monster Chaney plays here is a tough guy with a heart of gold in the tragic father-and-daughter tale The Road to Mandalay *(1926).* OPPOSITE: *As Quasimodo, Chaney cringes from Esmeralda's kindness, which he will come to repay a hundred-fold during the course of* The Hunchback of Notre Dame *(1923).*

THE ROAD TO MANDALAY *(1926):*
Chaney created the look of blindness for his role as a gang boss by spooning egg whites into his eye.

THE UNKNOWN *(1927): To appear armless, Chaney wore a straitjacket done up so tightly that his arms were not noticeable even when he was costumed in silk.*

LONDON AFTER MIDNIGHT *(1927): To make his vampire eyes bulge, Chaney tied a microthin wire around his head and over his eyelids. Animal teeth completed the effect.*

THE HYPNOTIST *(1928): Chaney used wires to distend his eyelids.*

Chapter Two

UNIVERSAL'S GOLDEN AGE

German writers relate that aside from impaling his victims, Dracula decapitated them; cut off noses, ears, sexual organs, limbs; hacked them to pieces; burned, boiled, roasted, skinned, nailed, and buried them alive; exposed them to the elements or wild animals. If he did not personally drink blood or eat human flesh, he compelled others to practice cannibalism. His cruel refinements included smearing salt on the soles of prisoners' feet and allowing animals to lick them for indefinite periods. If any relative or friend of an impaled victim dared to remove the body from the stake, he was apt to hang from the bough of a neighboring tree. With the cadavers of his victims left at various strategic places until beasts or the elements had reduced them to bones and dust, Dracula terrorized the entire countryside.

—The personal habits of the real Dracula (a.k.a. Vlad the Impaler), the role model for the novel and film vampires ever after. From *In Search of Dracula*, Raymond T. McNally and Radu Florescu, 1972

*This famous fugitive
(Boris Karloff) is literally
armed and dangerous, as
he faces his prosthesisless
attacker (Lionel Atwill) in
Son of Frankenstein (1939),
the sterling sequel to
Frankenstein (1931).*

IMPORTS

By the late twenties, radio was booming. MGM was showing Hollywood that the talkie wasn't a passing thing. The horror silent was in trouble and needed an infusion of new blood. That infusion came from Germany.

Following in the fantastic footsteps of visionaries like F. W. Murnau and Robert Wiene, director Fritz Lang was breaking new ground with the granddaddy of all psycho-killer pictures, *M* (1931), starring the menacing, moonfaced Peter Lorre. Lang had also made the grandmommy of all science fiction films, *Metropolis* (1926), a story about the horrors of a mechanized utopia. (A visit to New York City inspired Lang to make the film.)

In the United States, German-born Carl Laemmle had founded Universal Pictures in 1912, and as German filmmakers left a starving and economically crippled fatherland, they found a home waiting for them in sunny southern California. One such filmmaker was cameraman Karl Freund. By the late twenties, Freund had lent his creative vision to seemingly every major horror film that came out of Germany's famous production company, *Universum Film Aktien gesellschaft* (UFA). He had pioneered subtleties in lighting and fluid camera work that were perfect for setting the unsettling moods for horror films, and was one of the early directors to employ the innovation of color photography in his films. He had had a taste of Hollywood, and of Universal in particular, during his visit to the 1923 filming of *The Hunchback of Notre Dame*. Encouraged by his

And you thought punching a clock was bad! A weary worker finds himself at wit's end in a subterranean section of Fritz Lang's visionary **Metropolis** *(1926).*

Peter Lorre first wormed his way into the hearts of horror fans as a sweet-faced child murderer, Franz Becker, who likes to whistle a tune from Peer Gynt *as he satisfies his cravings in Lang's* M *(1931).*

colleagues, he moved his considerable genius and considerable bulk (he often weighed close to three hundred pounds [135kg]) across the Atlantic in 1930.

Freund made good upon his arrival at Universal by suggesting the unforgettable ending of a soldier's hand reaching for a flower, with fatal consequences, to *All Quiet on the Western Front* (1930). Laemmle was impressed with his cameraman and had Freund behind Universal's cameras for six pictures in Freund's first year at the studio. One of those six became one of the greatest horror classics of all time, vaulting its director, Tod Browning, and star, Béla Lugosi, to dizzying heights of fame, which subsequently led to the undoing of them both.

I AM DRACULA.
I BID YOU WELCOME.

Bram Stoker's bloodsucking aristocrat had seen a number of incarnations since the legendary actor Sir Henry Irving had premiered in the London stage play in 1897, but none were quite like what Hollywood was about to dish out in 1930. The director for *Dracula* was Tod Browning, who was no stranger to the strange. At sixteen, Browning ran away from home to join the circus, where he worked as a clown, contortionist, acrobat, and ringmaster. The circus was followed by a vaudeville stint, then Hollywood. Hollywood brought him success as a comedy lead, but Browning soon found that he favored the other side of the camera.

As his directorial and writing career progressed, Browning gained a reputation for the macabre through his work with the late Lon Chaney, whom he had directed in *London After Midnight*, in which Chaney played a vampire with what looked like a mouth full of shark's teeth. Like many earlier Hollywood horror films, *London* managed to twist itself into a happy ending: Chaney's vampire turned out to be a creatively disguised Chief Inspector Burke of Scotland Yard.

Browning's *Dracula* was released a year ahead of the Danish attempt to make a mark on the vampire market, with Carl Dreyer's *Vampyr* (1932). Based on Sheridan Le Fanu's short 1872 novel, *Carmilla*, *Vampyr's* vampire is a withered old crone who mysteriously drains a young girl of her life force. More atmospheric than horrific, the film has a timeless, dreamlike quality, aided by the fact that Dreyer shot every scene at morning or evening twilight through a piece of cheesecloth.

Browning was set to direct Lon Chaney again in the production of *Dracula*, but the actor's death made this impossible. Hollywood went looking for a replacement. Established film actors like Paul Muni were considered first, as was the German horror star Conrad Veidt. But a better choice—Béla Lugosi—was waiting patiently in the wings.

Born Béla Blasko in 1882 in the small Hungarian village of Lugos, a stone's throw from the count's Transylvanian stomping grounds in the Carpathian mountains, Lugosi was a decorated captain in the Hungarian Army. He was drawn to acting in Budapest, where his good looks and commanding personality landed him many classical leading roles, including Jesus Christ.

Hungary's failed communist revolution in 1919 made life difficult for Béla, who had actively supported the movement in hopes of making more work possible for actors. He dropped his last name and took on Lugosi, then moved to Vienna and then Germany, where film was thriving. By 1919, Lugosi had landed his first horror film role in *Necklace of Death*. Other roles followed, including F. W. Murnau's loose adaptation (sidestepping those royalties once again) of Stevenson's *Dr. Jekyll and Mr. Hyde*. However, the influential director's untimely death and the lack of work due to the Depression sent Lugosi packing once again, this time from Europe to the United States.

Lugosi knew no English and didn't intend to learn any. Forming a Hungarian stock company in New York City, he surrounded himself with fellow expatriates, but he soon found that the Hungarian theater market was limited. Luckily, a role in his first English-speaking play, *The Red Poppy*, brought him glowing reviews. One critic, Alan Dale, hailed him as "the greatest actor to come to America!" What Dale didn't know was that the Hungarian had memorized his part entirely phonetically.

Still, Béla's talent was undeniable. Throughout the mid-twenties, he fluctuated between film and theater, learning English but speaking with an accent you could still cut with a knife. On stage he played opposite Fredric March (who would win an Oscar for his 1932 Dr. Jekyll and Mr. Hyde in the film of the same name). On screen, he played the Eastern European heavy.

By 1927, with the horror play *The Werewolf* under his cummerbund, and a growing reputation for a certain sinister continental suavity, Lugosi got his big break. He was a natural for the play *Dracula*, which opened in New York on October 27, 1927, and ran for five hundred performances followed by two years of touring.

By 1929, Lugosi was in Hollywood, but so were the talkies: his ghoulish (goulash) accent was a big problem. His career pro-

HEY, STEVEN SPIELBERG! EAT YOUR HEART OUT!

Here are some marketing techniques suggested by Universal to promote Dracula's opening.

◿ **Distribute captioned publicity stills to promote household products.** An ad with Dracula on a cobwebbed stairway read: "The dust of centuries or the dust of today — clean them away with Gold Dust, Old Dutch Cleanser." An ad with Dracula poised above a sleeping damsel read: "Ah! She sleeps. Well, it must be an Ostermoor mattress."

◿ **Hand out Dracula bookmarks advertising the film's New York premiere.**

◿ **Have the novel Dracula read on the radio.**

◿ **Let the wind outside the theater twirl Dracula-shaped hangers, showing the count with cape outspread—front and back.**

◿ **Place signs by theater lobby mirrors, reading, "If you cannot see your reflection in this mirror, you are a vampire like Dracula!"**

◿ **Pass out "Dracula Is Coming!" doorknob hangers.**

◿ **Have ushers whisper the warning "Dracula is coming!" into the ears of patrons for other shows.**

◿ **Position nursing stations in theater lobbies just in case some members of the audience go into shock.**

◿ **Embroider Dracula on the capes of formally attired, wandering sandwich-board promoters with "DRACULA—It's Terrific!"**

◿ **Issue creepy masks to ushers for Dracula screenings.**

◿ **Write letters to local hospitals and doctors inquiring as to whether vampires really exist.**

◿ **Start a newspaper contest for "Write Your Own Ending for Dracula."**

gressed slowly until his performance in *The Thirteenth Chair* brought him to Tod Browning's and Universal's attention. Lugosi got a five-year contract and all the blood he could drink.

Dracula began production on September 29, 1930. (Strangely enough, a Spanish production for Mexican audiences was shot on the same set midway through production.) About forty-two days and $441,984 (several million by today's standards) later, the film was in the can. Though more faithful to the stage play than the Stoker novel—and a little stilted because of it—*Dracula* was a howling success with audiences. Universal's publicity department had whipped filmgoers into a frenzy of anticipation with an array of publicity stunts, including publishing a frantic telegram from Browning that begged the Foxy Theater in New York City not to open the film on Friday, February 13, 1931. Mercifully, the opening was moved up to February 12.

Although the film was chatty, Freund's photography in the early scenes was chilling. Browning's direction was as eerie and as atmospheric as always. The desolate, decaying stone interior of Dracula's castle was filled with scurrying rats, spiders, and a few inexplicable armadillos. (Browning's crew had even designed and built a handheld cobweb machine for him!) Lugosi's performance was towering, and generally agreed to be even better than it was on stage, for in the film he embodied the sinister and sexual to a perfect Transylvanian T.

Universal coveted Lugosi as their new Lon Chaney, but Béla was a marked man, even if he didn't know it. In an interview with writer John Sinclair a few months after *Dracula*'s release, Lugosi confided: "Circumstances made me the theatrical personality I am, which many people believe is also a part of my personal life. My next picture...will continue to establish me as a weird, gruesome creature. As for my own feelings on the subject, I have always felt I would rather play, say, Percy Marmount roles than Lon Chaney type of things.... I will never play the role of Dracula again."

But he did, though. Horror had trapped the proud, handsome Hungarian actor, who didn't network with the English-speaking power brokers of Hollywood and was a very shy man at heart. He did appear in a highly praised cameo opposite Greta Garbo in *Ninotchka* (1939), but the vast majority of the rest of his film life was spent on horror. How could you be taken seriously when fan letters asked if your parents were hypnotists, if you communed with ghosts, and why your eyes held an inhuman expression? Walt Disney went so far as to hire Lugosi to model for Satan in the "Night on Bald Mountain" segment of *Fantasia* (1939).

Among Lugosi's very best work were *The Murders in the Rue Morgue* (1932), the adaptation of Poe's story in which Lugosi plays the ape-loving mad scientist, Doctor Mirakle; *White Zombie* (1932), in which he embodies the Svengaliesque Monsieur Legendre, a

With hands like poised snakes and the face of a hungry fiend, Béla Lugosi gets ready to do a little dining out in the film that both made him a star and typed him forever, Dracula (1931).

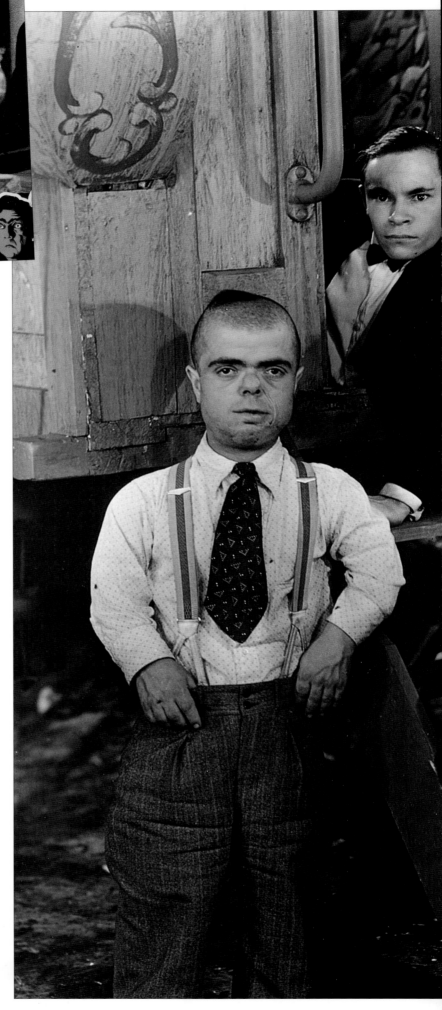

voodoo sorcerer; *Island of Lost Souls* (1933), an adaptation of H. G. Wells' classic *The Island of Doctor Moreau*, in which he plays a goat-turned-manimal; and *Son of Frankenstein* (1939), in which he stole scenes as the doctor's broken-necked assistant, Ygor.

Tragically, he appeared in many other films that were not worthy of his talents. The worst of these productions was his last, *Plan Nine from Outer Space* (1959), generally recognized as the worst film in history. After a long downhill slide, hastened by twenty years of morphine and methadone addiction, the count went down for the count on August 16, 1956. Horror had not been good to Béla Blasko. As he had said as early as 1933, "I can blame it all on *Dracula*. Since then Hollywood has scribbled a little card of classification for me, and it looks as if I'll never be able to prove my mettle in any other kind of role."

In the end, horror wasn't much kinder to Tod Browning than it had been to Lugosi. Spurred by the success of his vampire movie, he went on to make *Freaks* for MGM in 1932, a film many believe to be one of the most horrific of all horror films, and one that practically destroyed his career. *Freaks* harked back to Browning's early days with the circus, and was, in fact, scripted from an idea sparked by midget (and former Chaney costar) Harry Earles.

Love, lust, revenge, intrigue, and savage murder set in the circus was the basic plot. The cast was largely real: midgets, a legless man whose body stopped just south of his rib cage, a quadruple amputee who did everything with his mouth, pinheads, hydrocephalics, Siamese twins—all the "things" that Hollywood was fascinated by, but didn't want to see up close. Browning made these misfits his heroes, pitting the sympathetic freaks against a beautiful trapeze artist who marries a midget for his money only to betray him with the circus strongman.

ABOVE: A lesser-known Lugosi triumph, demented Darwinian Doctor Mirakle looks over his latest recipient for gorilla blood in The Murders in the Rue Morgue (1932). RIGHT: When macabre master Tod Browning (center) used the real thing for his fabled Freaks (1932) he wrote his own his ticket out of the Hollywood loop.

BLOODLINES

What if all the movie vampires assembled for a family photograph? Who might be related to whom? Just what might the bloodline be, so to speak? This chart tries to straighten out that thorny question.

Béla brings home the bacon to the magnificently constructed underground vaults of Castle Dracula.

Immediate Family

NOSFERATU

(1922/Germany/Prana): **The can opener–toothed patriarch and great-grandfather of all movie vampires. Based on Bram Stoker's novel, which was based on the life of Wallachian nobleman, supreme sadist, and possible blood drinker Vlad the Impaler.**

OLD DRACULA

(1973/Great Britain/World Film): **Dracula's dad, a classy old guy who drinks vintage blood saved up from skiing fatalities and other accidents from crystal glasses.**

COUNTESS DRACULA

(1970/Great Britain/ Hammer): **Dracula's mom, Countess Nasady, based on the real-life seven- teenth-century Hungarian countess Elizabeth Bathory, who from the age of forty kept her youth by bathing in the blood**

of virgins, occasionally showering in it when they were hung above her in an inwardly spiked iron cage. Bathory was eventually caught and walled up in her own bedroom.

DRACULA 1 *(1931/United States/Universal):* The favorite son and most famous of the brood. Has his father's continental charm (slightly different accent may be attributable to boarding school) and good looks, and his mother's taste for the sensual.

DRACULA 2 *(1958/Great Britain/Hammer):* The second son, Christopher. More like his father (even the accent) and the most proper of the lot. Good head for business and strongest stamina for remaining a blood-sucker. He has the Scars of Dracula *(1970/Great Britain/Hammer)* to prove it.

DRACULA 3 *(1974/United States/Universal):* The third of the four sons, Frank. Perhaps the sexiest of all the brothers. Has the unfortunate tendency to twist people's heads off and a problem with wobbling eyes. Believed to have been involved in a ménage à trois with Dr. Jekyll and Sister Hyde *(1971/Great Britain/Hammer).*

DRACULA 4 *(1992/United States/Columbia):* The baby of the bunch and an incurable romantic, Gary. Was a rebel ever since he ran away from home as a kid to join the Vampire Circus *(1971/Great Britain/Hammer).*

BRIDES OF DRACULA *(1960/Great Britain/Hammer):* Enough girls to go around for all those brothers. Some end up trading notes on challenges of married life with The Bride of Frankenstein *(1935/United States/Universal),* The Invisible Woman *(1941/United States/Universal),* and a woman who says I Married a Werewolf *(1961/Italy/Royal).* All have an antipathy towards the home-wrecking Frankenhooker *(1990).*

SON OF DRACULA *(1943/United States/Universal):* Dracula 1's son, Lon, who grows the mustache his father never could, spells his family name backward (ALUCARD), and moves to the swampland of Georgia. Monkeyed around with Son of Kong *(1933/United States/RKO),* Son of Godzilla *(1967/Japan/Toho),* and Son of Dr. Jekyll *(1951/United States/Columbia).*

DRACULA'S DAUGHTER *(1936/United States/Universal):* Dracula 1's daughter, who doesn't really want to follow in her father's footsteps, but finds that it's in the blood. Wears a hypnotic ring. Goes into therapy for her problem and falls for her therapist. Before therapy can help, she is shot in the heart with an arrow by a Transylvanian peasant. In a daughters-of-monsters support group with Frankenstein's daughter, who has already had a messy affair with a western outlaw in Jesse James Meets Frankenstein's Daughter *(1966/United States/Embassy),* Daughter of Dr. Jekyll *(1957/United States/Allied Artists),* and To the Devil—a Daughter *(1976/Great Britain/Hammer).*

Family Assets

HOUSE OF DRACULA *(1945/United States/Universal):* A drug-abuse clinic for monsters. The old Frankenstein Castle, where Dracula is medically treated for a blood parasite and the Wolf Man is treated for brain tumors.

ISLE OF THE DEAD *(1945/United States/RKO):* A Greek island but not the swinging Club Dead you might think. No falling asleep on a moonlit beach for Boris Karloff, who has to watch out for a vrykolaka (Balkan vampire).

BLOOD OF DRACULA'S CASTLE *(1969/United States/Crown):* The castle changes hands, and cousin John Carradine faces eviction from the old homestead.

LAKE OF DRACULA *(1971/Japan/Toho):* Lakeshore property never had such a steep price.

BLOOD OF DRACULA *(1957/United States/AIP): Dracula 1's granddaughter, a delinquent teenager who gets turned into a vampire by her high school chemistry teacher. Only understood by two other troubled teens, who say* I Was a Teenage Frankenstein *(1957/United States/AIP) and* I Was a Teenage Werewolf *(1957/United States/AIP).*

Family Pets

DRACULA'S DOG *(1977/United States/Vic): Zoltan, a Doberman pinscher, has teeth and then some. Not content with canned food. Frolics with Tim Burton's* Frankenweenie *(1992).*

THE DEVIL BAT *(1940/United States/PRC): Trained by Lugosi himself, this bat goes after shaving lotion given to executives at a cosmetics company.*

COUNT YORGA, VAMPIRE *(1970/United States/AIP): Lon's beefy ne'er-do-well son, who moves to Los Angeles, where he cruises the freeways for victims in a station wagon. Drive-By Suckings?*

MARTIN *(1978/United States/Braddock/Laurel): Pittsburgh teenager and fourth-generation Romanian (perhaps Dracula 1's great-grandson), who, while fangless, favors drugging and sucking his victims on trains. Has* The Hunger *(1983/Great Britain/MGM/UA) to be given bloodletting amulet by fellow fangless fiend, David Bowie. Won't even talk to wanna-be vampire Nicholas Cage about his* Vampire's Kiss *(1989/United States/Hemdale/Magellan Pictures). Last seen hanging out with* The Lost Boys *(1987/United States/Warner Brothers).*

INTERVIEW WITH THE VAMPIRE *(1994/United States/Geffen Pictures) Lugosi's bleached-blond great-grandson (Tom Cruise) has really been around and is about as good-looking as any vampire has a right to be. Lestat lives the high life in old New Orleans where life is one big, bloody party. But thanks to his bite-and-tell boyfriend, Louis (Brad Pitt), Lestat's frolics find their way into the tabloid press. How nineties can you get?*

Distant Cousins

EL CONDE DRACULA *(1970/Spain/Corona): A Spaniard and the oldest cousin.*

COUNT DRACULA *(1978/Great Britain/BBC-TV): French family relation, Louis Jourdan. Sexy enough to give Frank a run for his money.*

THE FEARLESS VAMPIRE KILLERS, OR PARDON ME BUT YOUR TEETH ARE IN MY NECK *(1967/Great Britain/MGM): A Jewish cousin who spurns crosses and sleds on his coffin.*

THE LEGEND OF SEVEN GOLDEN VAMPIRES *(1974/Hong Kong/Hammer): A cousin to the East in turn-of-the-century China. Look out! These suckers know kung fu!*

BLACULA *(1972/United States/AIP): African vampire Prince Mumawalde moves to Los Angeles, infects his girlfriend (if only he'd practiced safe sucking), and kills himself by walking into sunlight. Soul brother to* Blackenstein *(1973/United States/AIP) and* Dr. Black and Mr. Hyde *(1975/United States/AIP).*

DRACULA FAMILY TREE

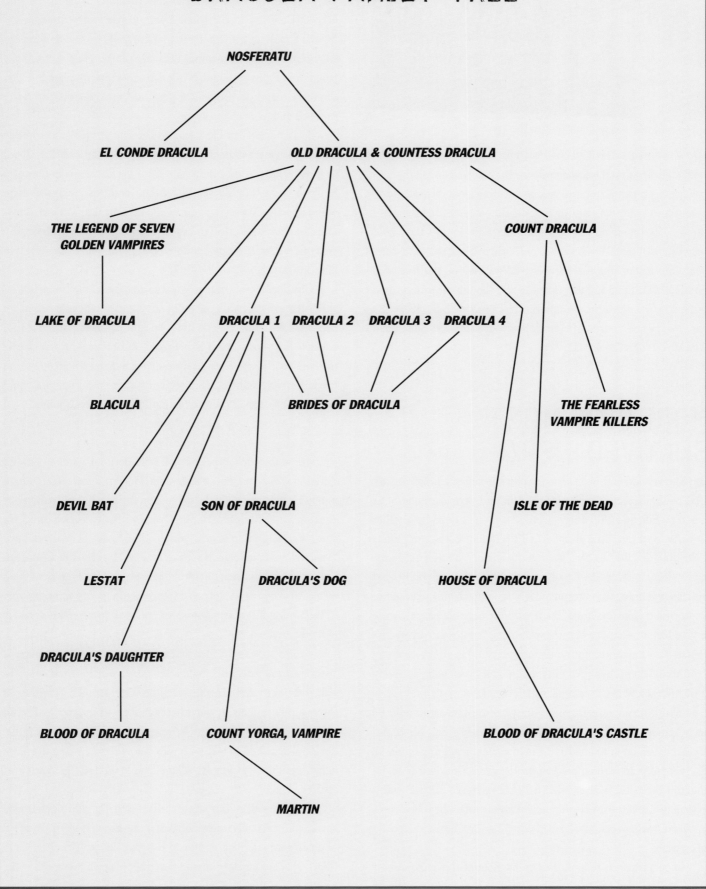

Lon Chaney wasn't the only actor who got to do drag in horror films. The distinguished Lionel Barrymore got his turn as the evil genius who could shrink any human into **The Devil Doll** *(1936).*

This turnabout would have been perfectly palatable, but the freaks' revenge on the evil couple in a final scene—with the normals cowering under a circus wagon in a thunderstorm as a swarm of murderous cripples squirm and drag themselves in for the kill through the mud, lightning illuminating the knives they hold between their teeth—was just too much for popcorn eaters to stomach. One of the biggest busts in MGM's history, the film was banned in England for over thirty years. Though Browning came back with a final horror masterpiece, *The Devil Doll* (1936), the experience had soured him on Hollywood. Likewise, Hollywood was happy to be rid of him.

HORROR'S MOST BELOVED HERO

Lon Chaney had also been slated to play the monster in Universal's 1931 production of *Frankenstein*, a film that was inspired not as much by Edison's 1910 silent original as it had been by another German original. Otto Ripperet's 1916 *Homunkulus der Führer* ("Homunculus the Leader") starred a monster who was, in a way, much closer to Mary Shelley's literary creation than the Hollywood version would be. This homunculus was no patchwork of criminal parts with a defective brain, but a brilliant, good-looking creature from a test tube, whose bitterness at being "synthetic" drives him to rise as a humanity-hating dictator until he is struck down by lightning. The prophetic quality alone, in light of what Germany ultimately spawned, is enough to chill the blood.

With Homunculus in mind, Hollywood went ahead with its own homage to Mary Shelley. As Lon Chaney's heir apparent, Lugosi was next in line to fill the monster's boots. Carl Laemmle, Sr., wanted Béla to play the mad doctor, while Carl Laemmle, Jr., thought the actor would make a better monster. Lugosi took a screen test, but the awkward makeup made him look like a cross between the Golem and a blob of dough, rather than a composite of corpses.

Lugosi was less than thrilled at the thought of playing a character that not only didn't speak (except in growls) but was also buried under mounds of makeup. (The only makeup he had allowed Universal's expert, Jack Pierce, to give him for *Dracula* had been a ghoulish, whitish green greasepaint.) He decided to pass on the monster, so Universal was back to hunting again. They found their Frankenstein in William Henry Pratt, who had left lofty diplomatic and governmental possibilities in London for North America and a life on the stage.

Boris Karloff, as Pratt was to become known, had already appeared in more than ninety films by the time he was considered to play Frankenstein. Born in 1887, he had made his way to Hollywood and Universal by 1917. At Universal, he progressed from being an extra to playing supporting villains, but work was anything but steady. Karloff dreaded returning to the backbreaking jobs and itinerant stage acting he had managed to subsist on in his early days.

One day, though, as he was trudging out of the Universal lot with fifteen cents in his pocket at day's end, a limousine came up behind him and honked its horn. Imagining an impatient mogul eager to put a lowly actor in his place, Karloff kept right on walking in the car's path. Eventually the back window rolled down and a familiar voice called, "Don't you recognize old friends, Boris?" The voice belonged to none other than the great Lon Chaney.

Chaney had hobnobbed with Karloff several times at the boxing matches they both regularly attended, and he liked the younger man's lack of pretense. That afternoon Chaney offered Karloff a ride home. For over an hour, the star asked about the bit player's ambitions and advised him on the film business. Perhaps sensing Karloff's despondency, Chaney tried to buck him up. He said, "If you're going to act—you're going to act. Even if you have to starve, never give up. It's the only way. The secret of success in Hollywood lies in being different from anyone else. Find something no one else can or will do, and they'll begin to take notice of you. Hollywood is full of competent actors. What the screen needs is individuality."

Karloff later said, "That talk with Lon gave me the courage to keep trying in later years when the going was far from easy." In 1931, he finally got his chance to be different. While eating in Universal's commissary one afternoon, he was approached by an assistant to director Frank Whale. Ushered to Whale's table, Karloff was asked to test for a role the next day. When the actor asked what the test was for, Whale simply replied, "for a damned awful monster."

There are differing stories about exactly why Karloff was selected. He himself maintained that it was because of his portrayal of a murderous prison trustee in Howard Hawks' *Criminal Code* (1931). But Béla Lugosi claimed that after his own test for the role, he had called Karloff to tell him that though "nothing," the monster might make the struggling actor some money. Carl Laemmle, Jr., in what sounds suspiciously like a press release, said later that Karloff's eyes got him the part. Laemmle claimed that his eyes "mirrored the sufferings of the poor dumb creature, in contrast to his frightful appearance and hideous strength." Others maintained that it was the interesting shape of Karloff's head that attracted Whale. Whether his gettting the part was due to his hat size, eyes, or talent, Karloff jumped at the opportunity.

Karloff's Frankenstein monster was an amazingly sympathetic character. As he said, "Whale and I both saw the character as an innocent one and tried to play it that way. The most heartrending aspect of the creature's life, for us, was his ultimate desertion by his creator. It was as though man, in his blundering, searching attempts to improve himself, was to find himself deserted by his God." Years later, he also graciously and unhesitatingly admitted, "The monster was indeed the best friend I could ever have. I was already well past forty and not getting any younger, and worried.... The part was what we call a natural. Any actor who played it was destined for success."

Any actor who played it was also destined for three and a half hours of merciless makeup application every morning, as well as an hour and a half of peeling, pulling, prying, and wiping with acids and oils to remove the makeup at night. By the time *Frankenstein* was underway, Karloff needed daily massage and infrared heat treatment to resuscitate his parched, makeup-covered skin, just to keep going.

A face that only a maker could love. Horror fans through the ages have stood in awe of this incredible collaboration of Boris Karloff's towering talent and Jack Pierce's makeup wizardry in Frankenstein *(1931).*

WHAT LON NEVER TOLD HIM

Boris Karloff owed a debt of gratitude and damnation to Universal's mad makeup scientist Jack Pierce for helping create the screen's most memorable monster. The following are some of the strange lengths that actor and creator went to in order to get that fabulous Frankenstein look.

Pierce dug through period anatomy books to find ways in which an amateur surgeon might cut into a skull. He determined that the doctor would have taken the easiest route, opening the top of the skull like a can—hence the monster's high forehead, staples, clamps, and scar.

Since the monster was a composite of easily acquired criminal corpses, Pierce read up on burial. He found that murderous criminals were often bound hand and foot and buried alive, and that as the rope eventually rotted and broke, it would cause a rush of blood that grossly enlarged both hands and feet, and even blackening the fingers. To create this effect, Frankenstein's sleeves and pants were made short and his finger tips were colored black.

Pierce experimented with skin color and finally got it right on the seventh try with a nice, dead greenish gray.

The bolts sticking out of the monster's neck were electrical input plugs. Pierce secured them so firmly that Karloff had tiny scars there for years afterward.

To slow his walk down to a monstrous shuffle, Karloff was fitted with steel struts to stiffen his legs. His feet were covered with two eighteen-pound (8.1kg) asphalt spreader's boots.

As Karloff wasn't particularly large, he had to wear a double-quilted costume throughout the shooting, which took place in the summer. He said, "I felt most of the time as if I were wearing a clammy shroud."

Pierce thought that Karloff's eyes seemed "too alive for anything that had only just been put together and not born, so to speak," so he hooded them with glued strips of rubber and wax. This invention was especially tormenting to remove.

When the film was released, Boris was not exactly treated royally, as Universal considered Colin Clive (Dr. Frankenstein) to be the real star. In fact, the end credits don't list Karloff: the monster's portrayal is credited to "?". Karloff was not invited to the film's Santa Barbara preview, either.

It was this preview that spurred the producers to alter the original fiery ending so that the doctor could live to experience marital bliss. They also originally cut the scene in which Karloff's monster hurls a child to a watery grave. Karloff himself had insisted on that. When shooting the scene where the monster and little Anna take turns tossing flowers into a pond until they have no more, Karloff had wanted Anna to transform into a flower in the monster's mind, leaving him moved to place her delicately in the water, where she would unexpectedly drown. Whale insisted on having Karloff toss the girl from over his head. Karloff, whose success as the monster was due largely to the innocence he brought to it, protested: "By no strength of the imagination could you make that innocent."

OPPOSITE: No blushing bride, veteran English actress Elsa Lanchester jumped at the chance to wrap herself up in what many consider to be the very best of the Frankenflicks, The Bride of Frankenstein (1935). ABOVE: Karloff looks on as others cower to his power in the movie poster for his final Frankenstein film, Son of Frankenstein (1939). RiGHT: Bargain with the devil? Karloff (right) has a unique method for supplying medical science with coveted cadavers in The Body Snatcher (1945).

Made for only $250,000, *Frankenstein* rode the cape tails of *Dracula*'s success to box-office glory. Universal was now convinced that there was big money to be made in horror, and thus began the first cycle of the Golden Age of Horror. Two *Frankenstein* sequels starring Karloff followed the original: *The Bride of Frankenstein* (1935) and *Son of Frankenstein* (1939). Karloff always preferred the original, insisting that it was a big mistake to let him speak in the second and that the furs made him look ridiculous in the third.

The year after the release of the original *Frankenstein*, Universal heralded Karloff as the heir to Chaney's throne (so much for loyalty to Lugosi). Karloff then made ten films in twelve months. Teamed up with Karl Freund as director and the same writer who had adapted *Dracula* for Tod Browning, Karloff made another horror classic: *The Mummy* (1932). The discovery a decade earlier of Tutankhamen's tomb, along with the bizarre deaths that followed it, was manna for movie moguls.

As the ancient, love-hungry Im-ho-tep and as his sinister resurrection, Ardath Bey, Karloff gave a hypnotic performance that was as smooth and madly menacing as his previous monster was uncouth and innocent. This time, Pierce's desiccating makeup took eight hours to apply. The cooked cloth, wrapped in three directions around Karloff's body and caked with dried mud and glue, seemed to disintegrate in front of the camera.

For Karloff, the fates were far kinder than they had been to Lugosi. He continued to be cast in many quality pictures, including *The Old Dark House* (1932), in which he played a murderous mute butler; *The Body Snatcher* (1945), in which he teamed up with Lugosi as a cutthroat grave robber for visionary horror producer Val Lewton; and Lewton's *Bedlam* (1946), in which he was at his sadistic best as the keeper of an insane asylum.

Ironically, as Lugosi had passed on *Frankenstein*, Karloff let the bandage-wrapped role of *The Invisible Man* pass to Claude Rains, insuring the smoky-voiced actor his place in horror's pantheon. But horror never limited Karloff the way it had Lugosi. Although he suffered from severe arthritis, Karloff had made approximately 140 films by his death in February 1969, and a number of the films had been "horrorless." One of his last roles, made

at the ripe age of eighty-one, was in Peter Bogdanovich's 1968 film *Targets*, in which he played an aging horror star trying to make good. And Karloff had, indeed. As he quipped with characteristic charm: "My leg in a steel brace—operating with only half a lung— why, it's a public scandal that I'm still around! But as long as people want me, I feel an obligation to keep on performing. After all, every time I act, I provide employment for a fleet of doubles."

OTHER ICONS

The early and middle thirties were a glorious time to be alive (or more appropriately, undead) if you were working in horror films. Two of the best films from studios other than Universal were reworkings of film and literary classics (as were most horror films).

H. G. Wells' uncomfortably conceivable tale of a vivisectionist turned creator of men, *The Island of Doctor Moreau*, received a truly fantastic production with *Island of Lost Souls* (1933) from Paramount director Erle C. Kenton. The great Charles Laughton does a star turn wielding both bullwhip and scalpel as Wells' evolutionary iconoclast, Doctor Moreau. Banished from London medical circles for his bizarre experiments on dogs, Moreau populates a remote island with hundreds of animals torturously worked into something short of human form and keeps his miscreations under marginal control as a feared and loathed doctor-creator-god. The film, shot on California's Catalina Island, has the lush and potentially menacing feel of the deep tropics. Beast men fill the night with chants of "His is the House of Pain!"

The House of Pain is about to change ownership, as Doctor Moreau (Charles Laughton) gets mobbed in the terrifying finale of Island of Lost Souls (1933).

The elderly Wells denigrated the film as "a mutilation" of his novel, which may have had something to do with the way in which the film diluted the science of the book and gave its hero the distinctly Hollywood love interest of a "panther woman." But even Wells couldn't deny the chill created by the beast people turning the scalpel on Moreau in the final scene or the sinister and hairy presence of Béla Lugosi's satyrlike Sayer of the Law.

The Moonfaced Menace

A more sustained chill came from the American film debut of yet another foreign-born actor destined for true horror greatness, Peter Lorre. Perhaps one of the most intriguing men ever to frighten a screen audience, Lorre was born Laszlo Loewenstein in 1904 in Rosenberg, Hungary, a small village in the Carpathian Mountains. He left home at seventeen for Vienna, where he divided his time between starting one of the first improvisational theater groups and studying psychology with none other than Sigmund Freud and Alfred Adler.

Lorre eventually found his way into both German film and theater, where he played comedians and character parts. After a stint as a sexually frustrated student in a Berlin production of *Wedekind's Frühlings Erwachen* ("Spring's Awakening"), the actor came under the scrutiny of renowned film director Fritz Lang, who recruited him for the role that would bring him international fame. As the tortured child-murderer in *M* (1931), Lorre simultaneously conveyed malevolence and vulnerability in a way that few actors have ever matched. Many people have credited the frightening believability of the character to his clinical understanding of the human psyche.

Lorre filmed *M* by day and played a humorous lead on stage by night. After *M*'s release, his growing fame and the rising of Nazi power convinced the half-Jewish actor to emigrate. A few years later, in London, he was introduced to a former UFA assistant director named Alfred Hitchcock. Although Lorre's English consisted only of "yes" and "no," he chose his words wisely and laughed at all the jokes he sensed that Hitchcock was telling him.

Lorre's talent and diplomacy landed him a juicy role as the fanatical leader of a group of saboteurs in Hitchcock's *The Man Who Knew Too Much* (1934). One review claimed that Lorre was able to crowd his character with "dark, terrifying emotions without disturbing his pallid moonface." Lorre's face was indeed perfect for playing on-screen neurotics and psychopaths. His large, sensitive eyes could bulge with anger; his sleepy, lilting voice could snap to savage hysteria; he could play characters whose menacing intelligence underlied their seeming servility—in short, he was a whole new kind of monster for the screen (although he once said that all that was needed to imitate him were two soft-boiled eggs and a bedroom voice).

Wanting to capitalize on Lorre's talent, Columbia Pictures quickly contracted him to play a variety of roles. While he was

picking and choosing his scripts, Columbia loaned him out to MGM for Karl Freund's last directoral work, *Mad Love* (1935), an adaptation of Maurice Renard's French thriller *The Hands of Orlac*. The film had been shot in Germany by Robert Wiene ten years earlier, starring Conrad Veidt.

For *Mad Love*, Lorre shaved his head to play Doctor Gogol, a renowned but loathsome transplant surgeon who takes a nightly box at Paris' Théâtre des Horreurs, where acts of torture are simulated on performers and waxworks. The doctor soon becomes obsessed with a beautiful actress, but the catch is that she's leaving the theater to go on tour with her husband, the brilliant pianist Stephen Orlac (Colin Clive took off his Frankenstein lab coat for this one). When a train carrying Orlac wrecks, destroying his hands, Gogol comes to the rescue out of love for the actress. Gogol secretly grafts the hands of a recently decapitated, knife-throwing murderer onto the pianist's mangled wrists.

Well, some things the body remembers. Although Orlac's healed hands forget how to play the piano, they start remembering how good it feels to throw knives. To hurry his imagined competition along, Gogol tries to drive the musician insane. He stabs Orlac's estranged father to death, then dresses himself with

TOP, LEFT: Peter Lorre's first foray into the English-speaking cinema was his splash as a cornered spy in Alfred Hitchcock's thriller The Man Who Knew Too Much (1934). ABOVE, RIGHT: As the brilliant, lustful, and lethal Doctor Gogol in Mad Love (1935), Lorre poses here with the object of his desire.

ABOVE: *Claw-shredded clothes—what could they possibly mean? Simone Simon (right) isn't sure she wants to know in the Val Lewton–Jacques Tourneur classic* Cat People *(1942).* **OPPOSITE:** *The movie that gave felines a bad name, while shorter on blood than the poster would suggest, was dripping with sexual tension.*

robotic arms and a sadistic-looking neck brace to convince Orlac that he is really the recapitated murderer whose hands are now doing the killing for Orlac. Far-fetched as it seems, Lorre gives an impassioned performance as the brilliant, lovelorn psychopath, and the ironic twist at the ending ensures him an appropriate exit.

Lorre's wit was as memorable as his screen presence. While in England in the thirties, he received a piece of fan mail from none other than the Führer himself, Adolf Hitler. Hitler lavished praise on Lorre for his screen portrayal of murderers and asked him to come back to Germany to do roles for the Fatherland. Lorre's telegrammed reply was courteous but brief: "Thank you, but I think Germany has room for only one mass murderer of my ability and yours."

Reanimating a Dying Demon

The late thirties: with censorship problems, a world war to be fought, and Universal's golden age devolving into pale spin-offs of the great originals, horror was in bad need of new blood.

The genre got a brief but brilliant transfusion from another European-born visionary in the early forties. (American writer James Agee later called him "the most sensitive movie intelligence in Hollywood.") Born Vladimir Ivan Leventon, Val Lewton had been

> ### THE GOSPEL ACCORDING TO LEWTON
>
> *Now there are two kinds of horror films, in my opinion. One is the monster-type, where they shoot the works in the first reel and from then on it's all downhill. And the other is a very carefully built-up mood picture of terror where you never see the monster, the monster is all in the minds of the people. They're all obsessed with fears, and there are certain basic fears in everybody that can be dramatized.*
>
> **— Val Lewton**

brought to America from Yalta, Russia, at the age of seven. His aunt was the brilliant Russian actress Alla Nazimova; his mother became the head of MGM's foreign reading department; and Val followed their footsteps into arts and letters. Attending the Columbia University School of Journalism, he went on to publish sixteen fiction (including erotica) and nonfiction works, and toyed with publicity writing at MGM as well. A book on Russian Cossacks landed him work as David O. Selznick's editorial assistant. He rose quickly to story editor, then wrote his own screenplays, and by 1942 was running a production unit at RKO and creating low-budget horror films. At the time, RKO, reeling from the expenses Orson Welles had incurred on his projects, needed quick, easy money. Val gave the studio more (ticket sales and quality) and less (gore) than they had bargained for.

Val Lewton produced his first horror classic, *Cat People*, in 1942. Directed by Jacques Tourneur (son of filmmaker Maurice Tourneur), the film was the first of a string of psychologically oriented projects that relied more on the implied than the impaled for their fear quotient. *Cat People* (remade and steamed up by Paul Schrader in 1982 for Universal) tells the story of Irene, a fetching New York fashion designer living with a strange fear and repressed desires.

Irene believes she is descended from a race of Balkan women cursed to transform into panthers when sexually aroused. The result: she won't consummate her marriage with her new husband, because there's no telling just how feral the nuptials might become. (Ads for the film read, "Kiss me and I'll claw you to death!") It's also never clear whether she really is a shape-shifter, as her face doesn't grow hairier in the mirror, no fangs sprout, and no eyes roll to the moonlight. (In fact, the big cat connection was so ambiguous that RKO insisted on inserting a shot with one.) Instead, the chills come from the fleeting form of insidious shadows and sounds—a panicked run through Central Park, a stalked swim in a basement swimming pool, a shredded bathrobe, and cat shadows made by Tourneur's fist. A little over budget at $134,000, *Cat People* grossed $4 million at the box office that year, earning enough money to pull RKO up substantially into the black.

Lewton and Tourneur followed their success with what has to be the weirdest *Jane Eyre* adaptation ever made. *I Walked with a Zombie* (1943) was based on a series of investigative newspaper articles from reporter Inez Wallace. This film details the journey of a private nurse who is hired by the owner of a tropical plantation in Haiti-like San Sebastian to nurse his strangely mindless wife—who might be a zombie—back to health. Here, the horror is just hinted at, and less is more, as night shadows and night sounds are

TOP: *Some of the stark and shadowy beauty to be found in Lewton and Tourneur's decidedly unsettling* I Walked with a Zombie *(1943).* **ABOVE:** *Lewton and Tourneur's* The Leopard Man *(1943) gave boys a turn at discovering the beast within.*

again used to expert effect. However, there is nothing remotely ambiguous about the mounting tension as nurse and mistress take a night walk through San Sebastian's cane fields to get a witch doctor's help. The scene is unnervingly silent, save for the wind in the reeds and the mounting throb of voodoo drums. The walleyed zombie guard (played by Darby Jones) whom they meet at a crossroads looks enough like the genuine article to make a believer out of anyone.

In 1943, Lewton and Tourneur also made *The Leopard Man*, in which a reporter goes to an isolated New Mexico town to investigate a series of mauling deaths that may have been caused by a leopard...or something else. Again, the menace is sensed rather than seen. The film's most frightening sequence involves a little girl forced to take a night walk across town and back to do shopping for her mother. On her return, she is pursued, and before her mother can answer her frantic pounding on the door...blood seeps under the sill.

Writer DeWitt Bodeén, who had collaborated with Lewton since *Cat People*, remembers how exacting the producer was: "Val was a marvelous producer, but then he attempted to do too

Placed in the same Upper West Side New York neighborhood as Rosemary's Baby *(1968),* The Seventh Victim *(1943) opened the door to decades of devil cult movies.*

much. He tried to move into every department, which was unfortunate. Val was the only producer, in the American sense of the word, to whom the credit *producer* really applied. People gave him credit for the whole thing, and in a way they're right. It's just that it became impossible for Val to work with anybody, and he couldn't do it *all* by himself....he wanted his hands on everything."

Lewton was demanding of the people who worked for him and frequently butted heads with the studio brass. The heart attack he suffered in the mid-forties made him even more sensitive to opposition. He did what he wanted to do and was increasingly convinced that the front office was out to kill him. Bodeen remembers being in the midst of researching *Cat People*'s sequel, *The Curse of the Cat People* (1944), when Lewton wrote him with a minor change in plan: "When you come back [to New York] you're going on to a story for *The Seventh Victim* because we've discarded the story you originally wrote. I've already put Charles O'Neal [Ryan's father] on it and you'll be working with him." Another letter asked Bodeen to go to a devil worshiper's society meeting. Bodeen attended under a pseudonym, and what he found was right up Lewton's alley: he found no grotesques slavering around a fire, but "mostly old people and they were casting spells on Adolf Hitler while they knitted and crocheted."

Bodeen and Lewton put the humanly sinister to work in *The Seventh Victim* (1943), in which Kim Hunter (*Planet of the Apes*) looks for her missing sister in New York's Greenwich Village, where she finds that her sibling was involved in a satanic cult, the Palladists, that drove her to suicide. Though the film was both a box-office and critical bust, it rings eerily true today in light of Jonestown, the Branch Davidians, and other true cult stories.

In the mid-forties, the increasingly perfectionistic Lewton teamed up with the venerable Boris Karloff to make three final classics. The first was an adaptation of *The Body Snatcher* (1945). The second film, *Isle of the Dead* (1945), was inspired by a Böcklin painting and a Goya sketch. Finally, there was *Bedlam* (1946), which was inspired by William Hogarth's engraving of Saint Mary of Bethlehem's Asylum and details the horrific abuse of the mentally ill in eighteenth-century London. Karloff and Lewton got along wonderfully. The horror king later called him "the man who rescued me from the living dead and restored my soul." Lewton's own soul was laid to rest after a second heart attack, in March 1951. He was forty-six.

One other true horror classic was made in the early forties: *The Wolf Man* (1941). This film helped second-generation horror actor Creighton Chaney (Lon, Jr.) rise to stardom and proved to be a thematic turning point for the genre itself. Creighton had been enjoying a successful career as a plumber up until the early thirties. His father, Lon, had never tried to make film acting attractive to his strapping son. (Creighton rarely visited on the set. After all,

it wasn't good public relations for a movie star to be seen with a big, gangly kid. It reminded studio officials of how old their hot property was, and Chaney was well into middle age.) When asked in 1928 about the possibility of an heir to the Chaney dynasty, Lon said, "He's six feet two inches [155cm] tall. That's too tall. He would always have to have parts built around him. He couldn't build himself for the part. Besides, he's happy in business and he's got a great wife." However, with the Great Depression, Creighton's plumbing business went out of business, and by 1932 he had begun taking bit parts in musicals, westerns, thrillers, and serials. Still, the going was lean enough to make him do the one thing he had sworn he never would—trade on his father's name.

Though Lon Chaney, Jr., got his big break with a nonhorror film, there was something a little horrible about the role. In *Of Mice and Men* (1939), he costarred with Burgess Meredith as Lennie, the child in a giant's body who has a penchant for beans 'n ketchup and for stroking soft living things (all too often breaking their necks in the process).

RKO saw young Chaney's monster potential in that film, and planned to line him directly under his father's shadow in a remake of *The Hunchback of Notre Dame*, but veteran Charles Laughton won the role. Young Chaney was also supposed to star in Universal's reprise of *The Phantom of the Opera*, but a very visible Claude Rains beat him out there. Sharpening his canine teeth as a scarred prehistoric patriarch in *One Million B.C.* (1940), Chaney finally garnered a serious contract with Universal, who put him into the role of a sideshow freak turned murderer in *Man-Made Monster* (1941).

Fortuitously, that same year, Chaney finally found a part he could sink his teeth into: the Wolf Man, horror's first innocent victim and monster rolled into one. *The Wolf Man* had no literary prototype to follow, but the myth of lycanthropy and shape-shifters had abounded in Eastern Europe for centuries. The film's writer, Curt Siodmak, had carte blanche in terms of the script, the result of which was a film about an all-American boy in wolf's clothing. The plot: Larry Talbot, a college student, is bitten by a werewolf while on a moonlit stroll at his family's ancestral estate in Wales. He beats the beast to death with a silver-headed cane, but soon begins to feel and dream disturbing things. An old gypsy tells the dream-troubled lad that he has been fanged by none other than her werewolf son (a "bit" part played by Béla Lugosi, who had gotten over his fear of makeup). The rest of Talbot's tale is as irrevocable as the old gypsy's rhyme:

> Every man who is pure of heart
> And says his prayers at night,
> May become a wolf when the wolf bane blooms
> And the autumn moon is bright.

To play the shape-shifter, Lon, Jr., put in makeup time that would have done his daddy proud. Actor Henry Hull, in Universal's previous attempt at lycanthropy for the screen, *The Werewolf of London* (1935), had kept monster-makeup master Jack Pierce at bay, submitting to only minimal makeup (he did wear a tail). The movie had been far too tame for horror-hungry audiences, so Chaney's werewolf was made to look much scarier, a process that took six hours. Specifics included a wolflike snout, yak hair painstakingly applied to Chaney's face a few strands at a time, a thick wig, and feet and hand coverings—and this was for long shots only. For the

close-up of the initial transformation itself, twenty-one makeup changes and twenty-two hours of stop-and-go filming were required; the shooting was done in reverse, with a little more makeup coming off with each setup. On the set, director George Waggner had the curtains behind Chaney starched so they wouldn't move in the mere seconds of time in which the change occurred. Chaney's hands had to be kept particularly still, too; the actor later claimed that his hands were nailed in place to a black background with tiny pins that actually pierced his skin.

Nonetheless, Chaney's star never rose to match his father's for inventiveness or charisma. While a fine actor in other genres, he may not have been true monster material. His "Son of Dracula" had a physique more akin to Captain Kirk or Batman. After all, just how scary could a slightly chunky vampire be?

Increasingly clunky, low-budget vehicles that chunky, old Lon, Jr., and other horror stars had to squeeze into became the unfortunate trend through much of the forties. With the world fighting a real monster in Germany and then feeling on top of the world after defeating him, Hollywood wasn't focusing a lot on the fantastically grim and grisly. The blossoming genre of film noir was by far the more popular way to communicate darker sentiments artistically. Besides, at the end of World War II, with the population shift to the suburbs, returning veterans making up for lost time with their work and families, and developments in television programming (another monster in its own right), movie attendance started declining in general.

In England, horror was experiencing even leaner times. Increasingly puritanical, British censors had stamped the scarlet letter of an "H Certificate" on the genre, effectively banning production from 1942 to 1945. The loss of that major foreign market made Hollywood studios even more cautious and lackluster in their horror-film output.

The fifties eventually revitalized the creature feature with a new brand of postwar and politically paranoid Hollywood techno-horror. The home front got attacked from below by hideously mutated creatures and from above by merciless invaders from outer space. By the sensual sixties, England's Hammer Films broke through censors' codes with sumptuously colored, sexually charged spin-offs from Hollywood horror classics. Again, actors such as Christopher Lee and Peter Cushing donned the bloody mantle of the horror star (and found it just as difficult to shed as their predecessors had). Great, grisly, graphic times lay ahead, and when they came, monster movies were a little more savvy and a lot less innocent than they had been in the golden age of the thirties. The glorious past was undead and buried.

LEFT: Lon Chaney, Jr.'s (left) finest hour may have been as his portrayal of the giant idiot child-man Lennie in the 1939 film version of John Steinbeck's novel Of Mice and Men, but his best-remembered portrayal was as the Wolf Man (OPPOSITE), shown here cringing before the bane of a silver-headed cane.

Chapter Three

SCIENCE HAS ITS PITFALLS

When he penetrated the bushes, he saw there were about twenty men, and they were all in exactly the same nightmarish state: their faces were wholly burned, their eyesockets were hollow, the fluid from their melted eyes had run down their cheeks. (They must have had their faces upturned when the bomb went off; perhaps they were anti-aircraft personnel.) ....One of them said, "I can't see anything."

—John Hersey, *Hiroshima*, 1946

That train is southbound, as the atomic octopus built by special effects maestro Ray Harryhausen wades ashore in the classic creature feature It Came from Beneath the Sea (1955).

By 1945, one madman, espousing the pseudoscientific theory of a super race, had exterminated six million Jews—roughly two-thirds of Europe's Jewish population. On August 6, 1945, one American plane dropped instant inferno on 100,000 people in the Japanese city of Hiroshima, leaving tens of thousands more to die of its poisons and still more to suffer hideous deformities in the next generation. On August 9, a second plane rained approximately one-half of the same death on the city of Nagasaki. By October 15, Winston Churchill had rung out a warning of the growing communist menace behind the "Iron Curtain." Within a few years, the United States would be fearfully hunkered down for a decades-long Cold War against this "evil empire."

For Hollywood, horror had taken on a whole new meaning by the end of the forties. The double-edged sword of technology was riper for grim reaping than it ever had been before, with super weapons out of science fiction soon to be globally poised for mass destruction. Scientists were starting to be feared as well as revered. And year by year, hysteria was growing over a distant culture that hungered to take over by outright conquest or subversion. The same paranoia had already stripped 120,000 loyal American citizens of their inalienable rights, simply because they looked Japanese.

The studios had no shortage of fear to play on.

MONSTROSITIES FROM THE PAST AND THE BLAST

After World War II, the impact of the atomic bomb had crept into the public consciousness. Conjecture was rampant over radiation's sinister possibilities. Had we created an uncontrollable monster? Could atomic blasts transform God's earthly creatures into humanity's nemesis, or would they waken the earth's long-slumbering, prehistoric giants to wrathful action against their reckless inheritors?

Stranger questions had been asked and answered before. After all, something had already stirred up giant lungfish from the ocean's depths into African fishing nets in 1938—and those hideous creatures were supposed to have been extinct for sixty million years. Only two generations earlier, supposedly prehistoric fifty-foot (15m) squids with suckers measuring a colossal fourteen inches (35cm) had washed up on America's Atlantic shores. The Abominable Snowman supposedly had roamed the Himalayas, and Loch Ness had its own living legend. Who knew what was out or down there?

The Jurassic Park *(1993) of its day,* The Lost World *and Willis O'Brien's marvelous stop-action models wowed plenty of moviegoers in 1925.*

Prehistoric monsters had long been music to movie-makers' ears. In 1912, D. W. Griffith made *Man's Genesis*, a journey back in time to the dinosaur age. But it was Marion Fairfax who adapted Sir Arthur Conan Doyle's classic adventure novel into the first major dinosaur silent, *The Lost World* (1925). Under Harry O. Hoyt's direction, Professor Challenger (Wallace Beery) returns to London from an expedition to a hidden plateau deep in the jungles of South America, with a brontosaurus egg ready to hatch. Naturally, the Royal Society lifts its nose at his preposterous find. Just as naturally, the dinosaur hatches, grows rapidly, and to spite the snobs, runs amok—all thanks to the stop-action model work of special-effects

pioneer Willis O'Brien. The brontosaurus' destructive romp through London was one of the first of many such cinematic antediluvian stomps through a major metropolis.

New York got its chance to get immortalized and immobilized in 1933, with the first truly classic big-creature feature: *King Kong* (originally called *The Beast*, the film was later renamed *The Eighth Wonder*, then stripped down to *Kong*, and finally expanded to its

With apologies to Elvis, there is only one undisputed king— and here he is, with arms almost long enough to reach off- shore in the classic King Kong *(1933).*

present title. RKO can hardly be faulted for groping for superlatives: Kong was pretty big).

This film, ironically about moviemaking, featured an ambitious director named Carl Denham, played with Barnumesque bravura by Robert Armstrong (although apparently modeled after the film's coproducer, Merian C. Cooper). Denham has big plans to shoot a movie on Skull Island. He has picked up a map of the place, rumored to contain prehistoric creatures on the prowl. Keeping this little secret to himself, he rounds up crew and talent.

The crew comes in the Gary Cooper mold of taciturn, explorer-hero Jack Driscoll (Bruce Cabot). The talent comes in the form of down-on-her-luck actress Ann Darrow (the world-class screamer Fay Wray). Together, the team boards a steamer for the uncharted tropics. Skull Island turns out to be an ancient place where dwellers have erected a huge wall to keep something out of their village. That something is precisely what Denham has come to capture on film. Unfortunately, when the villagers see Ann in all her blonde glory, they select her as the next bride-sacrifice (though not likely to qualify as a sacrificial virgin) to their living god outside the gates.

The rest really is motion-picture history: stealthy outrigger canoes making a kidnap by night from the sleepy steamer; Fay in chains; the race to save her amid throbbing jungle drums and chants of "Kong!"; that huge sliding bolt across the fortress gate; and finally, a quarter of the way into the film, the appearance of the big ape himself. Glibness aside, the building of the suspense, the atmosphere, and the real fear is hard to deny, even sixty-odd years later.

Of course, Kong himself was no giant, but another of stop-action photography wizard Willis O'Brien's magnificent models. The Kong doll was a steel-skeleton creation covered in black rabbit fur that was only eighteen inches (45cm) high. O'Brien's stop-motion animation shot Kong a frame at a time against tiny modeled jungle and city backdrops. For scenes where the love-struck monkey held Fay in the palm of his hand, a huge mechanical arm and head, covered in bear hide, were additionally used.

Surprisingly, reaction shots on the face of O'Brien's model are quite expressive. Kong, like Frankenstein, is a much misunderstood monster, as his feelings for his miniature bride seem to be pure. Luckily or unluckily, shots of Kong's huge feet as they squashed the fleeing villagers were cut from the final product.

O'Brien dominated the science-fiction and horror special effects field through the thirties and forties. By the fifties, he had passed his mantle to a successor, Ray Harryhausen. O'Brien had hired Ray as an assistant during the filming of Kong's more benevolent cousin, *Mighty Joe Young* (1949). Harryhausen went on to stop-animate dozens of horror and adventure films, including *The Beast from 20,000 Fathoms* (1953), *Twenty Million Miles to Earth* (1957), *Mysterious Island* (1961), *Jason and the Argonauts* (1963), and the immortal *Clash of the Titans* (1981).

In 1955, Harryhausen and director Robert Gordon unleashed one of the earliest screen monstrosities inspired by the atomic

bomb. The pair also gave movie monsters a new metropolitan center to destroy: San Francisco. *It Came from Beneath the Sea* pits a brainy but beautiful woman scientist up against a huge, mutant octopus. It seems that H-bomb tests in the Marshall Islands (where real tests had actually mutated islanders) had slithered their poisons to the unfathomable chasms of the Mindanao Deep. There, the poisons infected an octopus, who, for reasons of mutation or budget, possessed only five tentacles (each tentacle on the lifelike model is said to have cost ten thousand dollars). Naturally, the octopus, cursed with the double whammy of megagrowth and a fish-alienating radioactivity, starts feeding not only on Siberian seals but the Japanese fishing fleet.

The United States takes little notice until an atomic submarine gets tangled up with "It," and takes action only when "It" takes out a tramp steamer and starts raiding Oregon beaches for stateside snacks. After an arduous battle, "It" is driven back into the sea by flamethrowers and dispatched by the very submarine it tangled with in the first place.

Consequently, giant, radiated monsters became a horror staple of the fifties. Almost every species got its turn to terrorize. *The Beginning of the End* (1957) tells a story of radioactive isotopes introduced to enrich farm soil. Vegetables fit for giants result, but grasshoppers feeding on the produce grow just as big and descend upon Chicago. Ants, too, get a chance to destroy in the classic 1954 film *Them*, in which an atomic blast in the New Mexico desert sends "Them" west in search of sugar and blood sugar. The ants eventually make a new colony in the Los Angeles sewer system. Here, the horror of hugeness gets an added edge from the creepiness of collective insect intelligence.

In *Attack of the Crab Monsters* (1956), now-famous horror master Roger Corman gave his crustaceans the bizarre ability to speak

OPPOSITE: The scale between beauty and the beast may be askew (Fay Wray was much smaller in the movie), but the romance and terror are perfectly proportioned in King Kong. ABOVE: If you think the giant tarantula looks bad, you should see what the superglandular tissue growth serum has done to Doctor Deemer (Leo G. Carroll).

THE INCREDIBLE
SHRINKING MAN

starring GRANT WILLIAMS · RANDY STUART as APRIL KENT · PAUL LANGTON · RAYMOND BAILE
Directed by JACK ARNOLD · Screenplay by RICHARD MATHESON · Produced by ALBERT ZUGSMITH · A UNIVERSAL-INTERNATIONAL PICTUR

in the voice of anyone whose head they had recently nipped off and ingested. Leo G. Carroll unleashed a one-hundred-foot (30m) -tall, cattle-eating tarantula (1955) in the film of the same name, and one of Willis O'Brien's final flings, *The Black Scorpion* (1959), sent a colony of the giant poisonous bugs down from a volcano to invade Mexico City.

Nor were humans spared the tortures of radical size change. When a plane crashes on the site of the first plutonium bomb, the film's hero, Glen Langan, goes to the rescue, only to be transformed into *The Colossal Man* (1957). The flip side is just as ugly. A mad Lionel Barrymore (in drag, no less) shrank humans into tiny toys to do his evil bidding in Tod Browning's 1936 swan song to horror, *The Devil Doll*. *Doctor Cyclops* (1940) gave science another mad size-mologist, one who looked suspiciously Japanese.

In the best of the shrunken bunch, *The Incredible Shrinking Man* (1957), the main character, virile Robert Scott Carey, has the bad luck to be sprayed by a neighborhood pesticide truck and then drive a boat through a stray radioactive cloud. The result is more than a diet plan, and one to which *Thinner* author Stephen King owes a debt of thanks. Carey's torturous descent into the infinitesimal is believable, harrowing, and strangely poetic. Along the way, he suffers everything from feeling impotent (his oversize wife tries

LEFT: One of these monsters (the one with only one head) is Godzilla, the Japanese sensation and undefeated champ of all time, no matter how much hot air Ghidrah (1965) cares to expend on the subject. ABOVE: Nice kitty! As laughable as the lad might look, The Incredible Shrinking Man (1957) is so well done it will send you straight to the bathroom scale for reassurance.

WEIGHING IN WITH HORROR'S HEAVYWEIGHTS

(Statistics compiled from **The Great Book of Movie Monsters** *by Jan Stacy and Ryder Syversten)*

Monster (Type)	Height and Weight	Special Features
GODZILLA (Tyrannosaurus Rex)	200' (60m), Hundreds of tons	Searing radioactive breath, with awesome teeth, tail, and feet
GIGANTIS (Tyrannosaurus Rex)	100' (30m), 100 tons (90t)	Breathes fire, attacks Tokyo, vanquishes giant prehistoric porcupine
GIGAN (Seatopian monster)	200', 200 tons (180t)	Looks like a huge chicken in samurai armor. Has razor fins on back, spikes down abdomen, lone spike atop head, deadly beak and curved horns around the side of face, and massive swordlike arms
KING KONG (Giant ape)	50' (15m) tall, arms 75' (22.5m) long, chest 60' (18m) in girth, mouth 6' (1.8m) wide, teeth 1' (30.4cm) thick.	Fond of women, fears flashbulbs
MEGALON (Seatopian monster)	200', 200 tons	Looks like a massive shrimp in samurai armor. Has plating all over, deadly geometric spikes for arms, razor teeth on all sides of mouth. Is able to spit explosive balls every five seconds, and can chew through anything
GHIDRAH (Hatched from meteor)	200', 150 tons (135t)	Three-headed, winged serpent that breathes fire. Has three horns on each head, big teeth, and facial hair
GARGANTUA(s) (Twin humanoids)	200', 100 tons	Twin giants; the brown one is good, the green one isn't. Are invulnerable to bullets but not lasers
GAMMERA (Prehistoric amphibian)	400' (120m) long, 300 tons (270t)	Giant flying turtle with fangs. Breathes fire and causes worldwide destruction

JET JAGUAR (Giant robot)	Grows from 7' (2.1m), 400 pounds (180kg) to 200', hundreds of tons	Good but corruptible man-made robot that is friend to Godzilla. Is made from 5-foot (1.5m) -thick steel, and flies. Has steel teeth, always wears a smile, and is an expert in karate and judo
MOTHRA (Giant insect)	As larva, 300' (90m) long, 100 tons. As moth, has a 400' wingspan and weighs 200 tons	Giant moth from Infant Island. Protective of tiny singing twins, has enormous white wings that create hurricane winds. A peacekeeper
SMOG MONSTER (Chemical)	200', hundreds of tons	Looks like a squashed tadpole. Made from garbage and pollutants. Becomes octopus-like. Its touch is toxic. Can eat anything
REPTILICUS (Dinosaur)	50', 50 tons (45t)	Danish dinosaur found in oil fields of Lapland that can reproduce itself from any body part. Storms Copenhagen
RODAN (Pterodactyl)	200', 150 tons. Has 500' (150m) wingspan	Underground H-bomb tests crack and flood a mine with radioactive water and unleash a mutated, prehistoric monster that flies at supersonic speed. Wings make lethal wind
YOG (Alien)	From weightless to hundreds of tons	Jupiter creature that can metamorphose into and expand any body it contacts
YMIR (Alien/Dinosaur)	Variable	A Venusian monster and dinosaur in one. Doubles its size every day. Rampages through Rome and is shot in the Coliseum

Ecoconsciousness spawned this nemesis for a Godzilla turned protector. Risking asphyxiation and annihilation to save Tokyo but destroying it in the process anyway, Godzilla wages an all-out war with Hedorah in Godzilla vs. the Smog Monster (1971).

to reassure him that as long as he wears his wedding ring, he's got her. Of course, the ring slips off immediately after she says this) to contemplating an affair with a midget, and from shacking up in a dollhouse where he's hunted by his house cat to battling a small spider for survival in the basement.

Meanwhile, in Japan, a country that had reason to be radiation-obsessed, beasts from the blast were king. In *The H-Man* (1959), men were literally nuked into slithering, poisonous, cannibalistic ectoplasm. But towering above all other mutants stood the often-challenged-but-never-defeated heavyweight champion of radioactive monstrosities (and perhaps the best-known Japanese screen presence next to Toshiro Mifune): Godzilla. (The name Godzilla comes from the blending of gorilla with the Japanese kujira "whale." Though *Behemoth, the Sea Monster* (1958) may have wrecked London Bridge and Big Ben, this was nothing compared to the havoc that *Godzilla, King of the Monsters* (1954) would inflict upon Tokyo...again, again, and again.

Godzilla was created as an answer to Harryhausen's *The Beast from 20,000 Fathoms*, in which a dinosaur thawed from the Arctic goes to visit his ancient breeding grounds, which just happen to be New York City. With director Inoshiro Honda and special effects man Giji Tsuburaya behind him, and actor Hruo Nakajima often inside him (the one-hundred-pound [45kg] suit, that is), Godzilla starred in sixteen films, pitting his radioactive breath and city-crushing feet against some of the biggest, baddest monsters of all time. Although during the film span of his reign Godzilla would evolve from destroyer to protector, poor Japan got ripped apart each time just the same. As a character in one of the films aptly exclaimed, "First Nagasaki, now I have to be in Tokyo when this happens!"

Of course, all previously manufactured big boys of the Paleolithic era have been blown out of the swamp water by the dinosaurs in Steven Spielberg's *Jurassic Park* (1993). From the Jeep-chasing T-Rex to kitchen-stalking Velociraptors to poison-spitting Dilophosaurs (which never existed), the design team of Muren, Winston, Tippett, Lantieri, Industrial Light & Magic, and others have made movie history with monsters that even the most jaded horror fan wouldn't want to be any more real. Surviving through

Kauian hurricanes and budget battles, these dino designers perfected the art of terrifying illusion. In the famous raptor-in-the-kitchen-with-the-kiddies scene, who could tell that three dino operators with remote controls were crouching under the terrified children, with six more under the camera, and another twelve hiding in the kitchen cabinets?

MAD SCIENTISTS AND EVIL GENIUSES

With all this technology gone astray, some scientist had to be at the control switch...some scientist who wasn't playing with a full deck. His intentions might be noble (as Christopher Walken's were in the 1983 film that foreshadows virtual reality, *Brainstorm*), mixed (like the doctor who needs fresh faces to graft onto the daughter he disfigured in a car crash in 1959's *Les Yeux sans Visage*), or base (like Peter Lorre's sex-obsessed homunculus in 1935's *Mad Love*). Whatever his motives, the scientist always gets in over his head.

Most demented doctors of science owe a debt of gratitude to Rudolf Klein-Rogge for his unkempt and demented performance as the evil robotics genius Rotwang in Fritz Lang's 1926 masterpiece *Metropolis*. Lang's New York–inspired film portrayed an A.D. 2000 netherworld of machine-enslaved workers who lived beneath Metropolis' glittering surface. It is there that Rotwang (who sports one shiny rubber glove) creates the sexy robot duplicate of a chaste union maid, who whips the workers into such a frenzy that they flood their own city.

Of course, before celluloid, there was paper and ink. In 1886, Robert Louis Stevenson provided the literary prototype for the sinister scientist. "The Monster" may have been the star of Mary Shelley's *Frankenstein*, but master and monster shared the same dressing room in *The Strange Case of Dr. Jekyll and Mr. Hyde*.

> *It's going to do lots of things. Wonderful things. People who can't walk will be able to climb mountains. Blind people will see what nature looks like. You could go to faraway places and never go outside. Someday this machine might allow doctors to complete their whole medical schooling in one afternoon. You might even finish the seventh grade in a few minutes.*
>
> **—Christopher Walken, Brainstorm**

The tale began as a middling story of straight horror, but Stevenson's wife convinced him to burn the first draft and rewrite man and beast into one character in order to expose Victorian society's veneer of humanity. As a longtime invalid suffering from tuberculosis, Stevenson had often yearned for a life of physicality and instinctual behavior to match his active cerebral existence. This desire helped form the basis of Dr. Jekyll's frame of mind.

Though the popular book has been the springboard to more than twenty-five film and television productions (including star turns by John Barrymore, Spencer Tracy, Conrad Veidt, Boris Karloff, Jack Palance, David Hemmings, Michael Rennie, Kirk Douglas—even Jerry Lewis), the best of these was Reuben Mamoulian's Academy Award–winning 1932 version starring Fredric March.

March literally flung himself into the role. While some critics scorned his portrayal of Hyde as a racist creation (something that says much more about the critics than Wally Westmore's de-evolutionizing makeup), the film is a work of artistic and technological genius. The film opens with Jekyll at the organ playing J. S. Bach's "Toccata in D Minor," the same ditty of which the Phantom of the

> *Now, you who have sneered at the miracles of science. Now, you who have denied the power of man to look into his own soul. You who have derided your superiors. Look! Look!*
>
> **—Fredric March, Dr. Jekyll and Mr. Hyde**

Opera was so fond. The first several minutes of the film consist solely of Jekyll's ambling point of view and set a tone for visual innovation throughout.

Maddened by sexual frustration (an enforced eight-month engagement), Jekyll is driven to free his pleasures-of-the-flesh-seeking other half after an incredibly steamy encounter with a battered prostitute, played with very few holds barred by Miriam Hopkins. (In fact, the scene in which the nude "Champagne Ivy" pulls Jekyll down to her bed was erotic enough to be cut by Hollywood censors.) Afterwards, as the distraught Jekyll drinks his draught in front of a mirror, the transformation is something to behold.

In later years, Paramount guarded the secret of how it achieved the first seamless moments of March's metamorphosis, which was done through the removal of a series of red and blue

filters, consequently revealing layer upon layer of transforming face paint. The addition of peltlike hair, awful teeth, and bestial makeup was smoothed with dissolves. The transitions were covered by both the manic 360-degree spinning of the camera and a blur of sound effects, which included Mamoulian's own escalating heartbeat.

The scratching, twitchy, energized creature revealed bears resemblance to neither star nor doctor. Jekyll's posture, his movements, and even the cadence of his voice are altered completely. By the time March's murderous simian is caught, Mamoulian had set another standard for all clones to come. Unlike the book, in which Jekyll never regains his body, the film returns the monster to doctor in the peace of death.

Ever since, scientists have been losing their sanity. The wonderfully gravel-voiced Claude Rains got a dose of megalomania along with his translucency in Universal's 1933 adaptation of H. G. Wells' *The Invisible Man*. Directed by *Frankenstein's* James Whale,

ABOVE: Audiences went bug-eyed with horror for The Return of the Fly (1960), the sequel to The Fly (1958). RIGHT: Paranoid and power-hungry, Claude Rains has no mouth (or anything else that the eye can see) in The Invisible Man (1933).

We'll soon put the world right, now, Kemp. We'll begin with a reign of terror. A few murders here and there. Murders of great men...murders of little men. Just to show that we make no distinction. We might even wreck a train or two. Just these fingers round a signal-man's throat.

—Claude Rains,
The Invisible Man

ABOVE: William Hurt de-evolves to a primordial state in Ken Russell's hallucinatory story of scientific research run amuck, *Altered States (1980)*. **OPPOSITE:** It's a pity that this deaf-mute can't scream after she stumbles onto a bathtub full of blood and a little surprise—it's the only way she'll be able to kill "The Tingler" growing on her spine, before it kills her.

the film's effects are as marked by bravura as Rains' largely vocal performance. Cameraman John P. Fulton shot many of his visual effects against a background of black velvet, using a stunt man cloaked in the same material to manipulate objects. As crude as it sounds, the technique works like a charm, as does the stop-motion deathbed transformation from invisible man to dead mad scientist, thanks to dents in the sheets and the addition of bones, nerves, veins, and flesh. The only glitch is the shoe-prints-in-the-snow effect; this occurs when the Invisible Man is supposed to be barefoot.

Ray Milland does a twist on the invisible theme as Dr. James Xavier in 1963's *The Man with X-Ray Eyes*, playing a doctor obsessed with the vision's limitation of seeing only one-tenth of the full spectrum. The doctor develops an eyewash that soon lets him see through paper, wood, brick, stone, steel, and, ultimately, the face of God—after which he plucks out the little troublemakers.

Transformations, however, are not always as poetic. Ben Nye had designed glamourous makeup for Hollywood musicals such as *The King and I* (1956), *Oklahoma!* (1958), and *South Pacific* (1958), but his contribution to *The Fly* (1958) was something a little different. In the film, scientist Andre Delambre literally gets a bug in his matter transmitter while he's reassembling his own atoms. The result is a scientist with a fly's head and arm. The extensive makeup mask, which actor Al Hedison could thankfully unzip from the back, contained a clay proboscis, huge, multilensed eyes, and carved turkey feathers for feelers. A wig for the insect was provided by cosmetics giant Max Factor.

> *I turned into a small protohuman creature about four feet [1.2m] high. I followed a pack of wild dogs to the zoo....In the zoo I hunted down, killed, and ate a small gazelle. I was utterly primal. I consisted of nothing more than the will to survive, to live through the night, to eat, to sleep. It was the most supremely satisfying time of my life.*
>
> **—William Hurt, Altered States**

The ending here is a deliciously disturbing twist. With no hope for humanization, Delambre commits suicide by sticking his head in a steam press. Is the horror over? No. The film's final frames show a tiny fly with a man's head screaming for help as it faces consumption in a spider's web, which leaves the interesting question of who exactly got the fly's brain.

David Cronenberg's 1986 tongue-in-proboscis remake is even more disturbing. There are no switched body parts here, just a scientist, Seth Brundle (played by Jeff Goldblum) and his slow transformation into the unthinkable, beginning with a few coarse hairs on his back and culminating in a hideous creature that has to cover its food with acid vomit before ingesting it. As Brundle glibly tells his girlfriend (Geena Davis) before devolving into a savage yet savagely funny insect, "The computer got confused—there weren't supposed to be two genetic patterns—and it elected to splice us together. It mated us, me and the fly. We hadn't even been properly introduced."

Another contemporary, often hallucinatory tale of transformation is *Altered States* (1980). Adapted from a novel by Paddy Chayefsky (whose credits include *The Hospital*, *Marty*, and *Network*) and directed by the master of excess, Ken Russell, the film follows Harvard professor Eddie Jessup (William Hurt) as he takes the sensory deprivation tank places that even its inventor Dr. John Lilly could have scarcely dreamed of.

The supposition in *Altered States* is that humanity's long evolutionary climb is encoded in each human brain. With the aid of a sacred mushroom that gives each user the same primal memory/hallucination, Jessup "tanks up" to regress his consciousness to this primal scene. The catch is that his body regresses along with the hallucination. He escapes the tank and goes on to murder in the form of an anthropoid. Recovery only leads to the realization that, like Jekyll, his physical regression is no longer dependent upon either drug or tank. In hallucinatory sequences worthy of *2001: A Space Odyssey* (1969) (and aided with special effects from former *Exorcist* makeup wizard Dick Smith), Jessup is almost sucked down the evolutionary ladder into the primordial ooze from which humanity sprang. Only the love of a good woman saves him.

Though many twisted geniuses have leavened their dastardly deeds with humor, no one has done this quite like Vincent Price. A veteran stage actor and star of Roger Corman's campy yet classic American International Productions' adaptations of Poe tales such as *The Fall of the House of Usher* (1961), *Tales of Terror* (1962), and *The Tomb of Ligeia* (1964), Price also helped director-producer-promoter William Castle make his reputation in films such as *The House on Haunted Hill* (1959), *The Tingler* (1959), and *Thirteen Ghosts* (1960).

RIGHT: This wise audience member shows the proper technique for screaming during the demonstration sequence in The Tingler (1959). BELOW: Things get a little bit too hot to handle for mad sculptor Henry Jarrod, played by Vincent Price, in Hollywood's very first 3-D film, House of Wax (1953).

In *The Tingler*, Price plays a pathologist who is literally obsessed with fear. He discovers that the heightened emotion creates a jellied scorpionlike parasite at the base of the spine and only screaming can keep the creature from painfully killing its host. To prove his theory, he scares his deaf-mute wife to death in a nightmarish sequence that includes knife-wielding corpses, blood-running faucets, an arm reaching up from a blood-filled bathtub, and a display of her own giant death certificate. Castle, ever the showman, had movie theater seats wired to give off low-voltage shocks. This "percepto" effect accompanied a sequence in the film where a live "tingler" gets loose in the lab. Price's distinctive voice frantically urged the theater audience to vocalize: "Ladies and gentlemen, please do not panic, but scream. Scream

for your lives! The Tingler is loose in this theater. If you don't scream, it may kill you!"

Two of Price's most renowned madmen performances were as masked fiends, in *House of Wax* (1953) and *The Abominable Dr. Phibes* (1971). *House of Wax* was the apex of horror's dalliance with 3-D movies. As Henry Jarrod, Price plays the loving sculptor of a

> The end will come quickly now, my love. There is a pain beyond pain, an agony so intense, it shocks the mind into instant beauty. We will find immortality together, and they will remember me through you.
>
> —Vincent Price, House of Wax

ALL RIGHT, WHAT DID I DO THIS TIME?

While Boris Karloff might be most remembered for playing Frankenstein, he was most often the mad authority figure, medical or otherwise. Here's a sampling...with apologies to Tom Swift.

In **THE MASK OF FU MANCHU** *(1932), he rules as an oriental menace seeking Ghengis Khan's mask and sword, with which he will exterminate the white race and take over the world.*

In **THE GHOUL** *(1933), he's priceless as an Egyptology professor who returns from the grave, thanks to "the jewel of eternal light."*

In **THE BLACK CAT** *(1934), he's king of the hill as an Austrian engineer and devil cult leader, Hjalmar Poelzig, who has built his home on top of "the greatest graveyard in the world."*

In **THE INVISIBLE RAY** *(1936), he's hot as a radioactive scientist who can kill with a touch and melts a statue of one of the seven deadly sins each time he murders.*

In **THE MAN WHO LIVED AGAIN** *(1936), he scores as an old jealous scientist who transfers his brain into the body of his virile young rival.*

In **THE MAN THEY COULD NOT HANG** *(1939), he comes to life as a criminal surgeon who returns from the dead, thanks to a mechanical heart.*

In **THE APE** *(1940), he goes wild as a dedicated doctor trying to cure a polio patient and disguises himself in gorilla skins to stalk spinal fluid.*

In **BEFORE I HANG** *(1940), he's bloody brilliant as a kindly scientist working on life-restoring plasma who gets a transfusion from a condemned criminal and then kills...kills...kills.*

In **BLACK FRIDAY** *(1940), he has killer bedside manner as a doctor who controls a patient transplanted with a maniac's brain.*

In **THE DEVIL COMMANDS** *(1941), he really communicates as a lonely scientist who tries to reach his deceased wife with the help of a medium and hot-wired corpses.*

In **CORRIDORS OF BLOOD** *(1962), he's amazing as a drug-addicted anesthetist whose patients rise in the middle of surgery.*

In **CAULDRON OF BLOOD** *(1967), he's bad to the bone as a blind sculptor who uses fresh bones as the basis of his work.*

In **THE SORCERERS** *(1967), he's hypnotic as Professor Monserrat, who uses mind control on swinging young Londoners to experience their pleasures.*

In **THE SNAKE PEOPLE** *(1968), he's magical as Damballah, the voodoo cultist of a tropical island.*

wax museum who has been trapped in a fire that his partner has set in order to collect insurance money. Seemingly resurrected from the dead, Jarrod sets about not only destroying his old enemies but creating a new collection of waxworks with real bodies at the core. The best 3-D sequence is Jarrod's cloaked pursuit of a female model-to-be through the turn-of-the-century gaslit streets of New York. Later, when she strikes his face, his waxen life mask crumbles, revealing the charred psychopath beneath. For Price, the film was a true experiment in terror. As the 3-D process demanded two cameras mirroring each shot, there was no cutaway camera, so the actor had to do his own stunt work, including running under a collapsing three thousand pounds (1,350kg) of burning balcony.

Some of the promotional posters for Price's appearance in *The Abominable Dr. Phibes* show a beauty about to kiss a living skull, accompanied by the message that "Love means never having to say you're ugly," and it would have to be true, for Dr. Anton Phibes has been so disfigured that he can only talk, eat, and drink through artificial means. Yet when masked, he jauntily replicates the nine plagues from Exodus on the nine doctors he blames for his wife's death. The bizarre film includes a band of musical robots and Phibes embalming himself to the strains of "Somewhere Over the Rainbow."

Before his death in 1993, Price accepted his typecasting with the same class and humor he brought to everything else. "After all," he quipped, "you can't look a gift hearse in the mouth!"

Alien visitor David Bowie keeps his finger on the pulse of Earth culture by watching a little television in Nicolas Roeg's *The Man Who Fell to Earth* (1976).

TERROR FROM BEYOND

Some say the road to Earth is paved with good intentions. There are lots of reasons for "visitors" to stop by and say hello. Michael Rennie's Christlike Klaatu (and his robot, Gort) had to paralyze Washington, D.C., to get us to think about our homicidal tendencies in *The Day the Earth Stood Still* (1951). *This Island Earth* (1955) gave us the Metlunan, who merely wanted to recruit help to save his dying planet. David Bowie's performance in Nicolas Roeg's *The Man Who Fell to Earth* (1976) gave us an innocent from above to corrupt with our dirty Earth ways, while Andrei Tarkovsky's poetic space epic *Solaris* (1972) gave earthlings compassionate manifestations of their deepest yearnings. The main character in John Carpenter's *Starman* (1984) zapped himself into the body of a recently deceased housepainter and then proceeded to fall in love with his wife and this thing we call life on Earth. But most of the

time, E.T.'s cousins weren't here to take bike rides or steep themselves in the terrestrial experience. They were here to take over.

The monsters of horror's golden age threatened with their uncontrolled primalness, but the new breed of alien monster threatened to take that primal humanness away from us. We were ready for them, though; fighting off creatures from "out there" was good practice for the day when we would have to fight off comrades from "over there." Sometimes the invaders looked deceptively like us; sometimes they just looked horrible, and sometimes they didn't look like anything recognizable at all. To survive, we had to be very vigilant—and very paranoid.

Earthlings got their first shot at home defense against what has been benevolently described as an intellectual carrot. However, *The Thing (from Another World!)* (1951) was not your garden variety, lie-around vegetable. It liked blood and plenty of it. Howard Hawks, famed nonhorror director of classics such as *Red River*, *The Big Sleep*, and *Sergeant York*, produced the project and helped fledgling director Christian Nyby lens it. The film was based on the science-fiction novella *Who Goes There?* The film opens with a military and scientific expedition that results in the discovery of an alien spacecraft buried deep in the Arctic ice.

HORROR HAS ITS USES

There's more than one way to beat traffic at a stoplight. Monstermaker Lee Greenway was transporting his actor in full Thing makeup when a woman pulled up beside them, looked across, and fainted in her car. In fact, so many people in the first preview audience fainted at close-ups of the Thing that the film had to be stopped mid-reel.

Trying to free the spacecraft with explosives, the team blows it to pieces. Luckily, a large body is also found frozen nearby, so they don't go home empty-handed—though they soon wish they had.

Back at the base, the Thing, from which one of the team's huskies has already chewed off a carrotlike arm, is kept in cold storage until a squeamish soldier throws an electric blanket over it. The defrosted vegetable chews up the soldier and disappears into the Arctic night to stalk the installation. The rest is man against vegetable.

We rarely see the hulking, green-blooded vegoid for the rest of the film, but its presence is felt as it snatches sled dogs and crew members into the darkness. The team's scientific idealist mistakenly thinks there is something to be gained from communicating with his alien visitor and nurses little Thing spores, which turn out to thrive on blood, just like their father. With a vegoid army in the making and their heat cut off by the Thing itself, the crew is forced to flee to the generator room for the final showdown.

As standard as it sounds, the movie's last-outpost ambience and fine ensemble acting are a force to be reckoned with. The film also gave makeup artist Lee Greenway (and an actor who will remain nameless for the moment) a chance to create one of film's

Legendary Hollywood director Howard Hawks helped fledgling director Christian Nyby give audiences one of their first and best doses of Cold War paranoia by having monster horror meet science fiction in The Thing (from Another World!) *(1951).*

thanks to Francis Ford Coppola and Gary Oldman in *Bram Stoker's Dracula* (1992). Universal's other gruesome twosome, Frankenstein and the Wolf Man, are nipping at the vampire's heels, thanks to an unmistakable though disfigured Robert De Niro in Kenneth Branagh's Byronic *Mary Shelley's Frankenstein* (1994) and Jack Nicholson's womanizing, white-collar werewolf in *Wolf* (1994). Second helpings often pale in comparison to the first course, but this is not the case with John Carpenter's $15 million 1982 extravagant remake of *The Thing*.

The chilling story starts with a lone husky being chased and fired at over Antarctic wastes by a wavering Norwegian helicopter. The helicopter crashes before the dog can be dropped, leaving us to cheer for the innocent pup. Bad idea! The rest of the Norwegian facility is a charnel, and in keeping with the antagonist from the original novella, this Thing has the terrifying capacity to infect any organism, take over its body, and metamorphose when necessary. Its hunger to spread is insatiable and its transformations are almost unwatchable.

Thanks to visual magician Rob Bottin, who had made grotesque ghosts for Carpenter's *The Fog* (1979), the director scaled the heights of mind-blowing and at times lunch-blowing special effects. In one jarring scene, electrodes are hooked up to a recent fatality in the hopes of revival. Suddenly the corpse sprouts fangs, chews the doctor's arms off, stretches its neck down to the floor, wraps its tongue around a table leg, hoists the rest of itself off the

first space creatures. Greenway spent four months ferrying the Thing back and forth to Howard Hawks' home for a variety of design tryouts. What developed was an air-conditioned piece of makeup magic. A one-piece prosthetic fit over the actor's nose and cheekbones, around his ears, down his neck, and over his forehead. Football bladders were strapped around his chest and hooked up to ventilation tubes underneath the makeup and veins of colored water on the makeup's surface. As he breathed, the Thing both cooled himself and bubbled multicolored blood through the pulsing veins on his head.

Greenway also collaborated with Sinclair Paints to come up with a flameproof head for the Thing's fiery demise. This was one of the first times an actor had been ignited on the screen. As the flames subsided, Hawks' cameras dissolved from the original actor to a normal-size man, to a midget, to a model, all in Thing makeup, in order to show the shrinking alien.

Horror claims more recycled stories and remakes than almost any other film genre. Dracula has once more risen from the grave,

ABOVE: Time and again actor Gary Oldman has proved himself a master of metamorphosis. Never has he been so suave or so satanic as in Francis Ford Coppola's Bram Stoker's Dracula (1992). RIGHT: Another recent star turn of the monster variety has been Robert De Niro's stitch-faced performance in Kenneth Branagh's production of Mary Shelley's Frankenstein (1994).

Tapping the wellspring of anticommunism that flourished in the fifties, Invasion of the Body Snatchers (1956) featured Kevin McCarthy, shown here seeing his double.

slab, grows spider legs, and scuttles off (not a bad exit). One by one, the expedition team gets taken over or taken out. By the time the film is over, you don't know whether to applaud the two survivors or kill them as alien clones.

Hollywood had listened when comic-strip character Pogo said, "We have met the enemy and he is us." Science-fiction classics such as *Invaders from Mars* (1953), in which a boy's parents were aliens, and *I Married a Monster from Outer Space* (1958), with its suspicious spouse whose face takes on an alien look in lightning storms, carried the torch in a familial way. The more sympathetic *Strange Invaders* (1983) gave aliens a chance to bumble while cloning a whole town.

Real horror of dehumanization reached its height in 1956, under the expert direction of Don Siegel (of Clint Eastwood and Richard Widmark tough-guy picture fame) with assistance from Sam Peckinpah (the czar of gritty shoot-'em-ups such as *Bonnie and Clyde*). *Invasion of the Body Snatchers* tells the story of a small-town doctor, Miles Bennell (Kevin McCarthy), who discovers that his community and much of the rest of America have become replaced by clonelike pod people from another planet.

On the surface the film seemed as laughable as the science-fiction films, particularly with the film's campy beginning—just the type of trap Siegel intended to set for his unsuspecting audience. Before long, humor falls by the wayside, the pace and plot escalate, the enormity of the horror sets in, and the most paranoid film of all time is under way. What could be more horrifying than wondering whether your loved ones are really cold-blooded, emotion-

less monsters waiting for you to fall asleep so they can swap you for a clone developing in a pod? What could be more revolting than kissing the last person on Earth you trusted, only to taste something unfamiliar? What could be more terrifying than being chased by an entire town of disguised vegoids?

The paranoia is enough for a Freudian conspiracy theorist's field day, and Siegel's superb cast makes the most of it with almost no special effects. The film's bleak ending, with Bennell at his wits' end, scrambling through traffic to warn motorists of the invasion, proved so disturbing that Allied Artists decided to encapsulate the film with reassuring scenes in which the doctor is safely recovering in a hospital.

Philip Kaufman's 1978 remake of the film is a worthy and respectful successor. A ranting Kevin McCarthy is seen where we left him in the original, staggering through traffic, just prior to being crushed by a car before the eyes of this story's central characters, Elizabeth (Brooke Adams) and Matthew (Donald Sutherland).

The rainy maze of Seattle's streets, with their milling throngs of faceless people, is a perfect backdrop for alienation and distrust. The enemy seems as if it were everywhere. Like Matthew and Elizabeth, the audience finds itself gauging each new character for telltale signs of otherness. As Elizabeth says early on, "I keep seeing these people all recognizing each other."

The takeover feels unstoppable as clones carry out their body snatching with less and less secrecy. The heroes are ill-equipped lost members of the "Me Generation," complete with a pop psychologist played by Leonard Nimoy. The pod people play upon that consciousness in their nonviolent but merciless confrontations, mouthing soothing verbiage like, "You'll be born again into an untroubled world," and "There is no need for hate now...or love."

Horror plays both ends of the scale here. Furtive glances of terrified disbelief, inarticulateness in the face of panic, and the spied night moves of the aliens all make the film quietly believable. Meanwhile, the vegoids' transformations are almost as revolting as the acting is subtle. Giant pod flowers have pulsing centers that look like the gooey tops of emerging newborns. When a fleeing Matthew kicks a pod next to a sleeping bum and his faithful boxer, it develops into a disgusting dog clone with a man's face. As Elizabeth finally seems to collapse in Matthew's arms, a vacuum pump connected to a skull inside the foam-and-latex body that he's really holding sucks her into the shape of a shriveling pumpkin. The film's final twist is heart-stopping.

Of course, many aliens are terrifying, if not inexplicable, from the get-go. *The Blob* (1958) pitted teenagers against a jellied giant. *Day of the Triffids* (1963) brought us man-eating weeds with poison tentacles. You couldn't even see *The Andromeda Strain* (1971), but you dropped dead anyway. Yet ultimately, only one creature was unforgettable enough to make its movie its namesake.

When John Hurt gets his surprise-in-the-face from a pulsating pod after he ventures off the space freighter *Nostromo*, the manhunt is on in *Alien* (1979). Promotional advertising for the film may have read "In Space, No One Can Hear You Scream," but there was plenty of screaming in the theaters.

There was screaming in Hollywood, too. Dan O'Bannon's original script, which told of a carnivorous space stowaway, was bought and reworked by screenwriters Walter Hill and David

Giler—and the wrangle for credit began. But the finished story's uncanny resemblance to A. E. Van Gogt's novella *The Black Destroyer*, the pulp novel *The Voyage of the Space Beagle*, and the 1958 science fiction film *It! The Terror from Beyond Space*, which Roger Corman had already cannibalized in *Queen of Blood* (1966), soon had many Hollywood players up in litigious arms.

Though *Alien* is simply a stalk-and-destroy story at heart, director Ridley Scott's nightmare broke all sorts of barriers, particularly when it came to conveying a realistic atmosphere. The biomechanical, organlike looks of the deserted spaceship and desolate planet on which it was found, and the beast itself seemed completely alien, thanks to Swiss surrealist illustrator H. R. Giger. The production team of Roger Dickens, Carlo Rimbaldi (lovable E.T.'s creator), and Michael Seymour actually made the mechanized terror. Their baby grew from the creepy crustacean attached to John Hurt's face to the crazed snake exploding from his chest to the slimy yet skeletal, air-duct prowling, ever-growing killing machine with dripping jaws...inside of dripping jaws...inside of dripping jaws.

The *Nostromo* itself seemed somberly realistic as a glitzless, utilitarian vehicle. Perhaps most important, the heroine and final survivor was glitzless, too. A force to reckon with, Ripley (Sigourney Weaver) was as unlikely to scream at the sight of a monster as she was to have a mad, passionate affair with a fellow crew member. She set a standard for monster-challenging women that few have followed except herself in the two terrifying sequels, *Aliens* (1986) and *Alien III* (1992).

You might want to keep this list handy the next time you're lying in a field at night gazing up at shooting stars. Sure, it's nice to know that with democracy flourishing in so much more of the world, Hollywood's astronomical alien anxieties have been alleviated...at least a little. In Steven Spielberg's *Close Encounters of the Third Kind* (1978), aliens promised to give Richard Dreyfuss the ride of his life. By the time director John Sayles dropped *The Brother from Another Planet* (1984) into the neighborhood, the galactic visitor was a pretty cool dude. *Alien Nation* (1988), not to mention the television series by the same name, had the amphibious-looking creatures living, working, and getting high on milk products right alongside us. James Cameron's *Terminator 2* (1991) went so far as to have an alien (in the guise of everyone's favorite muscle-bound Austrian, Arnold Schwarzenegger) saving the human race. Still, there's no harm in keeping our terrestrial guards up. Especially when creatures from beyond have learned one of the most recent innovations of the twentieth century: political double-talk. If you run into a white-haired Herculean gent mouthing the politically correct sound byte "I Come in Peace" (1990), read between the lines...and put up your laser shield. As Attila the Hun would tell you, old habits die very hard.

A contemporary horror heroine is not someone to fool around with, as Sigourney Weaver's Ripley is ready to prove in the nerve-shattering **Aliens (1986).**

HOW CAN I KILL THEE?
LET ME COUNT THE WAYS.

Try to match up the movie monsters with the varied tools of their ultimate demise.

Movie Monster

1. Alien

2. The Andromeda Strain

3. The Blob

4. Cobra-Man from SSSSSSS

5. The Colossal Beast

6. Deadly Mantis

7. Demon from The Exorcist

8. Dracula

9. Ghidara

10. The Giant Behemoth

11. Giant Grasshoppers

12. Gigantis

13. Gigantua

14. Godzilla

15. The Golem

16. Gwangi

17. Invisible Invaders

18. It Came from Beneath the Sea

19. Jack Torrance in The Shining

20. Killer Tree

21. King Kong

22. Martians

23. Nosferatu

How to Destroy It

A: Water her

B: Get teenagers to surround them with a circle of cars and turn on the headlights

C: Let it get inside you, then throw yourself out the window

D: Make him a frozen minotaur in a maze of hedges

E: Scream!

F: Shoot the hilt of a knife blade that is embedded in its heart

G: Use the "Oxygen Destroyer," a weapon so terrible that its creators committed hari-kiri

H: Sick a hungry mongoose on him

I: Give it a giant overdose

J: Get his wife to talk him into remembering his former humanity, putting down the kids in the school bus, and grabbing those high-tension wires

K: Trap it while it's nesting in New York's Holland Tunnel from The Beginning of the End and bomb it with cyanide gas

L: Trap it inside a church and burn it down

M: Sucker it into a space pod and blast it out to oblivion

N: Get him to fight with his good twin and he'll slip into a volcano

O: Have Godzilla and Mothra fling him out to space

P: Give him a radium-torpedo enema

Q: Lure them into Lake Michigan with squeaky, chirpy sounds

R: Shoot it in the head with a harpoon torpedo

S: Send a kamikaze pilot crashing into a snowy mountain and bury the beast in an avalanche

24. Reptilicus

25. The Saucer Men

26. The Tingler

27. The Thing (from Another World!)

28. Triffid

29. Wicked Witch of the West

30. Wolf Man

The scientific crew of a North Pole U.S. Air Force base wonder what became of their recently thawed visitor from beyond and how they might kill him in **The Thing (from Another World!)** *(1951).*

T: Groove them to high-frequency sounds from **From Hell It Came**

U: Give him plenty of sunlight

V: Break his heart (with a stake) from **The War of the Worlds**

W: Club him with a silver cane

X: Shoot him off the Empire State Building

Y: Take away his Star of David

Z: Sicken them with the common cold

AA: Let time take its toll

BB: Zap it with electricity

CC: Blast it with fire extinguishers, freeze it, and dump it in the Antarctic

DD: Water it

Chapter Four

UNNATURAL NATURE, OR, JUST WHEN YOU THOUGHT IT WAS SAFE TO GO BACK INTO THE...

There is nothing as sweet as the taste of revenge.

—popular saying

This Gill Man wants out of the prison of his Florida tourist tank...and he'll get it in Revenge of the Creature *(1955).*

There was a time when man was a meal. In every cave the roulette game was the same after dark. Who would the local saber-toothed cat, that human flesh–eating machine of the Stone Age, drag off for its takeout dinner tonight? When would the screaming start? Feline feasting lasted through the millennia until man mastered the use of weapons (although he never lost his fear of the dark).

Among the first in our arsenal, as Stanley Kubrick's *2001: A Space Odyssey* tells us, were the bones of dead animals, animals we had killed as we slaughtered our way into the realm of thought. Charles Darwin claimed our top-dog position was simply the survival of the fittest, and tough luck to the rest. The Old Testament blessed humanity as the stewards of nature with "dominion over the fish of the sea and over the birds in the air and over every living thing that moves upon the earth." All in all, it's been quite a job being the king of the biological hill...and what a bang-up job we've done of it.

Now, let these images float through your mind for a second: fish floating belly-up in dead rivers, oil-slicked birds taking their last breath of Arctic air, whole families of minks skinned for a once-a-year coat, future drumsticks with their feet stapled to an abattoir's conveyor belt, rabbits blinded in the name of smudge-proof mascara, and bulldozers smearing whole species out of rain forests. Time for that snack, isn't it?

Okay, so we've let our minions down a bit. Still, one wonders, if our guilt or discomfort about endangering and destroying the natural world measures anything on the Richter scale of emotion, what seismic activity could the rage of our little furry, feathered, fishy, and feelered friends register?

Not much, because animals can't think or organize, right? But then how can ethologist Irene Pepperberg's African gray parrot, Alex, use a seventy-one-word vocabulary to express himself? How can a bonobo chimp named Kanzi possess the grammatical skills of a two-and-a-half-year-old human? How did Koko the gorilla learn to use sign language? How do wheeling flocks of birds know how to keep in faultless formation? How is it that ants are so organized that they seem to have a common mind?

Maybe we'd better rethink our position...before payback time begins—before the hunter becomes the hunted.

Lon Chaney, Jr.'s Wolf Man may have been the first monstrous animal to make us sweat silver bullets over taking a walk in the woods. Stephen Spielberg may have perfected the scare tactic when it came to a casual swim in the ocean. However, scores of films before and since have taken the previously benevolent and least aggressive parts of nature and made them a menace. Thanks to Hollywood, just about every warm- and cold-blooded critter that walks, crawls, flies, slithers, or swims has been unleashed on unsuspecting humanity. And they're not the only ones. Killer flora and machines have had their day on the silver screen, too.

WARM-BLOODED KILLERS

Alfred Hitchcock's dark masterpiece *The Birds* (1963) is a stand-out story of fowl revenge, and one of the most celebrated celluloid nightmares that filmgoers have ever flocked to.

It is never explained why all the birds around California's Bodega Bay have decided to turn on humanity; they just do it. From James Pollak's opening titles, each of which seem to be eaten away bit by bit to the accompaniment of snicking sounds, a vague feeling of dread pervades a seemingly harmless film. Though there are a few well-placed forebodings along the way, it's only after half a film's worth of sexually charged banter between lawyer Mitch Brenner (Rod Taylor) and socialite Melanie Daniels (Tippi Hedren, in her first film) that the screen erupts in terror. In other words, a giant mass of gulls inexplicably swirls through San Francisco; a lone gull grazes the heroine's head, another smashes itself into a schoolteacher's door; and the local chickens won't eat. Then all hell breaks loose.

Hitchcock had sensed that special effects were the coming thing, so he thrust himself into the vanguard, as he would so often, by planning a film whose budget would be used not on stars but on stellar technology. He had planned over fifteen hundred separate shots for the film—twice as many as was usual for most filmmakers and three times his normal count. (No wonder production designer Robert Boyle based his concept for the film on Edvard Munch's famous painting *The Scream*). Almost four hundred of the shots were trick shots of the avian invaders. Hundreds of live gulls, crows, starlings, and other birds were recruited, many under the expert training of Ray Berwick. Masses more of stuffed birds were obtained to fill out crowd scenes, such as the creepy congregation on the school jungle gym. Disney animators were employed to hand-paint sparrows on film for the scene where the birds flood in through an open fireplace. Double-exposed film of more birds was used in scenes such as the children's flight from school. In the end, $200,000 was spent in developing mechanical birds for this classic film.

For talent, Hitchcock ignored studio pressure to cast Anne Bancroft as Annie, a lonely schoolteacher, and put newcomer Suzanne Pleshette in the role instead. When model and television actress Tippi Hedren was invited out for dinner with Hitchcock's family and friends, she found a little box from Gumps of San Francisco at her place. Inside was a gold bird pin encrusted with

also excised a now seemingly far too lighthearted scene, in which Mitch and Melanie laughingly hypothesize about the flock's fearless leader while burning bird carcasses. Gone were the lines that might have made film history, "Birds unite, you have nothing to lose but your feathers."

Tippi Hedren had another predator on the set to worry about: her director. Not satisfied with controlling her at work, Hitchcock dictated to his starlet what she must eat, wear, and who she could see while off the set. When she rebelled, he went so far as to hire private detectives to follow her. As the stalwart Hedren later remarked, "He could be two different men. He was a meticulous and sensitive director who gave so much to each scene and who got so much emotion into it!—and he was a man who would do anything to get a reaction from me."

Granted, the character of Melanie was a smug princess who some filmgoers would love to see have her feathers ruffled. But Hitchcock's social skills included whispering obscenities to Hedren before emotional shots and sending her to the brink of insanity with shooting one of the most unendurable film sequences an actor would ever have to live through: the final air attack on Melanie in the attic. One minute of film took seven straight days of filming—and how many years of therapy?

In the original attic scene, Suzanne Pleshette was scripted to be the victim, but Hitchcock thought it more appropriate for his leading lady to get the attention. Hedren had been told time and again that mechanical birds were going to be the only creatures to fly into her face for this culminating scene. The cast had already filmed the final scene without birds. For the locustlike entrance of Disney's animated starlings, Hitchcock had brought a drummer to the set to simulate thousands of wing beats for the actors to flail

seed pearls. She took the bait and accepted the lead role. She had no idea what was in store for her. On the Pacific Coast north of San Francisco, the crew worked on the film for a year, the actors for six months. In twenty weeks of shooting, Tippi got one day of rest.

The birds were a little more than unruly. Though protected from human harm under the eye of the Humane Society, no organization protected the humans from the fowl. Berwick worked magic with his live charges, training them to swoop inches away from actors' heads on cue, perch, and then return when the shot was over. The crew had a little more to deal with. The birds were everywhere—on lights and props—and not easily moved. So many of the crew were scratched and bitten that tetanus shots were ordered for all. During filming, a local farmer's young lamb had been found with its eyes pecked out by crows. Hitchcock took the hint and had the film's matriarch, Lydia (Jessica Tandy), find a local farmer whose eyes were in the same condition. The legendary economist

ABOVE: In filming the grueling attic scene that put her in the hospital, Tippi Hedren almost succumbed to Alfred Hitchcock's The Birds (1963). RIGHT: This lobby card nicely captures the helpless feeling that pervades every frame of the film.

Socialite Melanie Daniels (Hedren) and young charges run from avian assassins in The Birds. Not everyone survives.

to. Hedren's solo part upstairs shouldn't have been much harder, but the mechanical investment had gone belly-up. The robots just didn't look real enough, and there wasn't enough time to create a whole new set of animations.

When Tippi arrived on the soundstage, she found the attic set surrounded by a cage of wire mesh. Inside were grim grips wearing heavy leather gloves, surrounded by crates and crates of very angry birds. There had been a slight change in plan.

Makeup master Howard Smit made up Hedren for the scene: "As she sat in my makeup chair, I covered her with bird pecks, blood, scratches, and bruises. She happened to look in the mirror for a moment and suddenly she pushed my arm aside and graciously said, 'Pardon me for a moment, Howard.' She ran outside and threw up." Makeup mishap aside, Hedren bore up admirably under the punishment she received for the next seven days. From angle after angle, bird after bird was hurled at her beautiful face. Visiting actors from Hitchcock's stable marveled at the young actress' toughness, but the going got tougher. Once Tippi had slumped to the floor during the attack, a new problem presented itself. The birds covering her prone, helpless body were flying away too quickly. Hitchcock's solution was to sew little loops into his star's costume in order to pin the angry birds to her body. Unfortunately, one bird got feisty enough to sink his beak into her left eyelid. Tippi, who ran screaming from the set, finally got a much-needed break from filming—a week's worth of medical recovery. As for Hitchcock, when asked about his treatment of the star, he quipped, "To paraphrase Oscar Wilde, 'You destroy the thing you love.'"

The final component of the director's dark vision was sound. As always, Hitchcock had waited to worry about that aspect of the film until after it had been edited. Composer Bernard Hermann (of *Psycho* fame) was called in to oversee the process. A radical concept was soon embraced: there would be no music at all. A score of natural and artificial bird sounds was devised by Hermann, Remi Gassman, and Oskar Sala, much of which was played on a synthesizerlike device called a trautonium. Trauma-tonium might have been a better name, for trauma is what this effect subliminally achieves, from the opening credits to the final menacing, white-noise-

> *Hitch on Handling Leading Ladies: "I always believe in following the advice of the playwright Sardou. He said, 'Torture the women!' The trouble today is that we don't torture women enough."*

> *Hedren on Hitch: "I had always heard that his idea was to take a woman—usually a blonde—and break her apart to see her shyness and reserve broken-down, but I thought this was only in the plots of his films."*

filled silence that greets Mitch as he cautiously carries a catatonic Melanie outside the besieged house to his car. As the hero, heroine, and family drive off in a long shot under a lowering sky, through what looks like an amalgam of all the winged things in creation, no reassuring credit rolls by to announce "The End," for the end is just the beginning.

Losing the Rat Race

Rodents are almost always sinister on-screen, at least when not depicted as the Country, City, Mighty, or Mickey Mouse type. Rats have a long and lethal rap sheet that dates back to the deaths of twenty-five million Europeans during the five years that the Black Death raged in the mid-fourteenth century. Rats also carry rabies, are capable of squeezing their bulk through tiny places, can chew through almost anything, are notoriously aggressive, have been known to gnaw on untended infants, breed with alarming speed, and are mankind's favorite subject for lethal experiments. In 1971, *Willard* provided a venue for rats to do a little experimenting of their very own.

In *Willard*, Bruce Davison plays Willard Stiles, a twenty-seven-year-old mama's boy with the social skills of, well, Alfred Hitchcock. Willard's late father's fortune is stolen by his unscrupulous boss, Mr. Martin (Ernest Borgnine), and the poor kid is thus condemned to a life as a ridiculed stockboy in the company he should have inherited. Martin has plans to snatch the family mansion from Willard and his elderly mother (the Bride of Frankenstein herself, Elsa Lanchester). With no one to turn to, the boy finds solace in the companionship of the lowly house rats his mother has sent him to exterminate.

Soon Willard is training fifty of the furry beasties. With the leadership of two capable squad commanders, the good-hearted Socrates and the too-bright-for-anyone's-good Ben, the rats are soon training themselves. Willard sends a rat army to trim his

ABOVE: As Stuart Whitman broods in the background, Hitchcock veteran Janet Leigh weighs a bunny that will, believe it or not, soon be terrorizing her Arizona town in Night of the Lepus **(1972). BELOW, LEFT: Getting ready for the charge on their master's belligerent boss, a cadre of highly trained rats menace Ernest Borgnine as Bruce Davison looks on in** Willard **(1970).**

employer down to size. "Tear him apart," is the only command necessary. While the effect is terrifying, there is a distinct impression of flying rats being flung at their victim.

Human love is the boy's undoing. Having fallen for Sandra Locke (who, ironically, went on to direct *Ratboy*, 1986), Willard sees the error in his ways and plots to poison his progeny. But Ben smells a rat, and in a cataclysmic final scene, the assassins chew through a door to murder their former master. The real star turns out to be Ben, who survives to find another master (and a hit song by Michael Jackson) for himself in the sequel.

In other films, less sinister critters have exterminated the exterminator. In the all-star (Samantha Eggar, Peter Cushing, Ray Milland, and Donald Pleasence) trilogy *The Uncanny* (1977), three killer kitties avenge their owners' murders. Ferociously hungry, five-foot (1.5m) -long Blarina shrews (played by Dobermans with fangs) take over a tropical island in *The Killer Shrews* (1959), directed by none other than *Gunsmoke*'s Festus (Ken Curtis). Perhaps most uniquely terrifying, are the monster rabbits in the classic B film *Night of the Lepus* (1972), which starred Janet Leigh (*Psycho*) and Stuart Whitman. Here, in response to farmers whose land has become overrun by pesky rabbits and whose coyote predators have been poisoned, scientists accidentally release a rabbit mutated to breed sterility into all the rest. Instead, its offspring are four-foot (1.2m) -high roaring carnivores who can jump hundreds of feet and have a taste for truck drivers.

Man's Best Friend

What could be more disillusioning than man's best friend becoming his worst nightmare? Just ask the relatives of the people killed by pit bulls in recent years. Sir Arthur Conan Doyle may have given us *The Hound of the Baskervilles*, but the 1959 Fox film was unavailable for years because of its reference to Sherlock Holmes' cocaine habit. With reported incidents of inbred saint bernards turning on their masters, it was only right for Stephen King to fill the gap by turning one of the loyal snow dogs into a slobbering savage through rabies.

Cujo. Remember that name: you don't want to call it. Director Lewis Teague added more hydrophobia to his massive mutt, so the film lacks the demented dog's-eye-view of the book. But the tale of 170 pounds (76.5kg) of canine pain and fury trapping an adulterous mother, Dee Wallace (*The Howling*, 1981), and her young son (Danny Pintauro) in their Ford Pinto for two days on a deserted farm one

blazing summer in Maine is confrontation at its most primal: Mom against the dog from hell. The slobbering, suffering, former good dog is fully capable of shattering windshields, and the humans inside are fully capable of dying from heat and lack of water.

Perhaps the most famous man-craving creature lay in wait for swimmers in the deep dark Amazon. But eating them wasn't exactly what he had in mind. He swam on the heels of Universal-International's 3-D success, *It Came from Outer Space* (1953), to become horror's first postwar superstar; one worthy of his own Aurora model right next to Frankenstein, Dracula, the Wolf Man, the Mummy, and the Phantom of the Opera.

In this film, spurred by the discovery of a prehistoric webbed hand, archaeological explorers board a questionable boat for the backwaters of the Amazon Basin. Their quest for the fossilized remains of a 350,000,000-year-old evolutionary missing link between fish and man turns up the genuine article, *Creature from the Black Lagoon* (1954).

Amateur astronomer John Putnam is about to discover why so many of his friends and neighbors (or are they?) have been acting strange in It Came from Outer Space.

TOO B, OR NOT TOO B?
THAT IS THE QUESTION!

Night of the Lepus *wasn't the most strangely named or the farthest-fetched, B horror flick to ever escape from the celluloid lab. Here is an indexed taste of other unusually descriptive titles and a hint at what weird wonders they contain. Coming to an insomniac near you.*

Film	What You're In For
THE ATTACK OF THE 50-FOOT WOMAN	A housewife zapped by a huge, lusty alien goes looking for her philandering husband
BARN OF THE NAKED DEAD	A maniac tortures women while a radiation-poisoned dad stalks the Nevada desert
CHILDREN SHOULDN'T PLAY WITH DEAD THINGS	Satanic rites on a tropical island
COLOR ME BLOOD RED	A successful artist paints with his own blood but needs more supplies. The ultimate sacrifice-for-your-art film
THE CORPSE GRINDERS	A cat food company staffed by crippled derelicts buys corpses from graveyards. The contented kitties become vicious
THE COUCH	An ice-pick killer enters analysis
DEAD EYES OF LONDON	A huge, bald, blind killer leads a gang of blind men on a rampage
DEAFULA	The first horror film in sign language
THE DEVIL'S DAFFODIL	Christopher Lee plays a Chinese detective in a German film
THE EARTH DIES SCREAMING	A test pilot returns to London to find robotic zombie masters in control
EUGENIE: THE STORY OF HER JOURNEY INTO PERVERSION	George Saunders graces this story of a virginal daughter trapped on a sadistic millionairess' private island
THE EVICTORS	Vic Morrow plays a lethal real estate agent
THE HORRIBLE SEXY VAMPIRE	A tale of reincarnation starring Waldemar Wohlfahrt
THE HOUSE OF PSYCHOTIC WOMEN	Three sisters and a murderer find themselves snowbound
HOW AWFUL ABOUT ALLAN	A serial killer falls in love with a nine-year-old
THE HUMAN VAPOR	Anthony "Norman Bates" Perkins is a semiblind mental patient released to live with his psychotic sister, played by Julie Harris

I DISMEMBER MAMA	A Tokyo bank robber on the run learns the secret of how to be "mist" by the cops
ILSA, SHE-WOLF OF THE S.S.	The Nazis' most secret weapon
THE INCREDIBLY STRANGE CREATURES WHO STOPPED LIVING AND BECAME CRAZY, MIXED-UP ZOMBIES	First monster musical. Vilmos Zigmond is cinematographer
INVASION OF THE BLOOD FARMERS	Resurrected Druids need blood to kindle their queen
ISLAND OF THE BURNING DOOMED	Aliens send a killer heat wave in the winter in order to make humans spontaneously combust
LEECH WOMAN	A woman lives off male hormones to stay young
THE MAN WHO HAUNTED HIMSELF	Roger Moore discovers his extroverted duplicate
MESA OF LOST WOMEN	Jackie "Uncle Fester" Coogan creates a superwoman with long fingernails
MURDER BY TELEVISION	Béla Lugosi as twins
THE NIGHT GOD SCREAMED	Jeanne Crain versus Jesus Freaks
THE NIGHT OF A THOUSAND CATS	A crazed millionaire feeds people to frisky felines
NO SURVIVORS, PLEASE	A reporter and secretary investigate aliens who are using the minds of murdered scientists
PLEASE DON'T EAT MY MOTHER	A soft-core version of Roger Corman's classic, Little Shop of Horrors
SATAN'S CHEERLEADERS	Cheerleaders use their evil powers to make their team win
THE SAVAGE BEES	Michael Parks (Then Came Bronson) attends Mardi Gras with killer bees
SPERMULA	Beautiful vampires from outer space suck something besides blood from their helpless victims
THREE ON A MEATHOOK	Talk about bad luck
THE TOOLBOX MURDERS	Crazed apartment super gets creative with a nail gun
THE WASP WOMAN	No, she doesn't play polo. She's the head of a cosmetics company who uses wasp enzymes to stay young...until she bugs out
THE WORM EATERS	A worm-eating contest was held at the Las Vegas premiere of this crawler

ABOVE: Richard Carlson is going to have his hands full protecting Julia Adams from the advances of the Creature from the Black Lagoon. RIGHT: Interracial dating may have been taboo in the fifties, but interspecies romance did fine at the box office. This missing link knows just what he's been missing.

Among the scientific party is Kay Lawrence (Julia Adams), who looks particularly alluring in her white swimsuit—to both her crewmates and the Gill Man, whose habitat she plunges into. In an underwater scene worthy of Esther Williams, the Creature swims just below his heartthrob, sensually mirroring her every move, even lovingly brushing her leg at the end of their aquatic ballet. Poisson passions drive him to kidnap Kay from the boat, and the battle for the beauty is on.

Horror veteran Jack Arnold's (*The Incredible Shrinking Man* and *Tarantula*) direction, James C. Haven's underwater photography, and swim champion Ricou Browning's dive into monsterdom are what make this film a classic. Bud Westmore and Jack Kevan's incredible Gill Man costume, which was said to have been mod-

eled on the Oscar statue, was no burden to Browning. With the use of an air hose, he could hold his breath for five minutes at a stretch during underwater scenes shot in Silver Springs, Florida. Ironically, the swimmer kept his fin in the biz and went on to direct episodes of *Flipper* in later life.

Cold-Blooded Killers

Film critic Vincent Canby may have called *Jaws* "a noisy, busy movie that has less on its mind than any child might have on the beach," but Steven Spielberg's 1975 film adaptation of Peter Benchley's thriller kicked box-office sand in the eyes of heavyweights like *The Sound of Music, The Godfather, Gone with the Wind,* and *The Exorcist. Jaws,* the father of all shark movies, boasted an all-star cast of modern Captain Ahabs (Roy Scheider, Robert Shaw, and Richard Dreyfuss), a giant shark that looked all too real (courtesy of Academy Award winner Bob Mattey, squid builder for Disney's 1954 *20,000 Leagues Under the Sea*), a simple yet unforgettable musical score by John Williams, and more water thrills than any adventure park in its right mind.

The Great White in this fable isn't a whale but two tons (1.8t) and thirty relentless feet (9m) of shark, which really should be down in Australia but decides to make Amity, Long Island, its summer chomping ground. Tourist-hungry local bureaucrats, tourists hungry for the ocean, something in the ocean hungry for the tourists—it all adds up to lots of blood. When the landlubbing police chief, Brody (Scheider), an impetuous shark specialist, Hooper (Dreyfuss), and a grizzled shark hunter, Quint (Shaw), set off to track the beast down, the hunters very quickly become the hunted.

Originally slated for a fifty-two-day shoot on Martha's Vineyard, Spielberg's budget became inflated and his schedule expanded to 152 days. The three twenty-four-foot-(7.2m)-long mechanical sharks were problematic and sometimes dangerous (the main shark was christened Bruce, later Brucette, when it had to be pregnant for *Jaws 2*), and actors and director snarled at each other, but the result vaulted them all into superstardom. The film also gave Robert Shaw one of the best entrances that an actor has ever had. In a town meeting that is reaching hysteria, his fingernails screech down a blackboard—next to the drawing of a man being eaten by a shark—to get everyone's undivided attention.

So did Shaw's speech about the true and tragic fate of the *USS Indianapolis*, torpedoed on June 29, 1945, while returning from delivering the atomic bomb to the Pacific during World War II. The secrecy-shrouded ship sank, leaving its bleeding crew treading water in shark-infested waters for five days. Eleven hundred men went in and 316 came out. Quint was one of them. Before long, it would be déjà vu time.

Jaws also spawned a school of killer fish movies to swim in its bloody wake. *Mako: Jaws of Death* surfaced the same year, as did *Shark Kill*, followed by *Tintorera*, *Tentacles*, and *Orca* in 1977. *Barracuda* and *Killer Fish* tried to take a bite out of the new market in 1978 and 1979, respectively, and *Great White* gave chase in 1981. Finally, in 1983, *Jaws 3-D* gave viewers more realistic views of shark vomit than any film in history.

If only our aquatic adversaries were content to remain at home in the ocean. In Steven Spielberg disciple Joe Dante's 1978 gut-and-water-churner *Piranha*, the adventurous little guys work their way to the inland United States. And, as it turns out, the piranhas are not so little, really, but a two-foot (.6m)-long, thirty-pound (13.5kg) superspecies bred as a booby trap for the Vietnam War and then brought back to North America only to be accidentally dumped just upstream of a summer camp. In this gory film, water sports take on a whole new meaning.

Independent filmmaker John Sayles, whose toothy script helped give *Piranha* its bite, brought life and humor to another pet gone astray in Lewis Teague's *Alligator* (1980). This time, Ramone, one of those lovable little reptiles that kids are forever buying and parents are forever flushing down the toilet, gets as big as a Cadillac in an urban sewer system, thanks to a twelve-year diet of industrial waste and corpses from animal experiments.

From the moment the body of a sewer worker named (yes, it's true) Ed Norton is found, this gator is almost unstoppable. It devours cops, reporters, and millionaires, breaks through sidewalks, lurks in alleyways, terrorizes pools, eats a Great White hunter, and even chews up a garden party before tough cop Dave Madison (Robert Forster) can track it down to the sewer's sinister blue shadowy depths and kill it with bomb-ignited sewer gas.

Swimming back to shore is tough when your leg has just been ripped off. So begins the relentless terror ride of Jaws *(1975).*

> As the light went, the sharks came cruisin'. We formed tight groups—somewhat like squares in an old battle— you know what I mean—so that when one came close, the man nearest would yell and shout and pound the water, and sometimes it worked and the fish turned away. But other times, that shark would seem to look right at a man—right into his eyes—and in spite of all the shoutin' and poundin', you'd hear that terrible high screamin' and the ocean would go red, then churn up as the shark ripped him. Then we'd re-form our little squares. By the first dawn, the sharks had taken more than a hundred. Hard for me to count but more than a hundred. I don't know how many sharks. Maybe a thousand. I do know they averaged six men an hour. All kinds—blues, makos, tigers, all kinds.
>
> —Robert Shaw,
> Jaws

All God's Killers, Great and Small

There really isn't one of God's little creatures that hasn't stood in line for revenge, Hollywood style, so forget taking your pet snake to science class. Mad scientist Strother Martin turns his daughter's boyfriend into a killer cobra in SSSSSSS (1973).

Forget digging for bait. An electrical storm charges up toothy bloodworms who neigh like horses and burrow through human flesh in *Squirm* (1976).

Forget reading *Charlotte's Web*. Poisonous spiders terrorize in the 1977 William Shatner vehicle *Kingdom of the Spiders* as well as his more recent *Arachnophobia* (1990).

Forget cute bumblebees. The little honey makers aren't very sweet in either British horror-maker Freddie Francis' *The Deadly Bees* (1967) or one of the most star-studded B pictures of all time, *The Swarm* (1978).

Forget the boric acid. That won't stop the man-eating cockroaches who can spell words with their bodies in William Castle's 1975 swan song to horror, *Bug.*

ABOVE: Some horror films are more prophetic than we'd like. In The Swarm (1978), killer bees waged war against a host of Hollywood legends, including Gloria Swanson and the here reclining Olivia De Havilland. BELOW: The entire ecosystem of a swamp takes revenge on a family in The Frogs (1972).

In one film, almost all the beasties come together for one mass attack. *The Frogs* (1972) advertised itself with the appetizing line, "Millions of slimy bodies squirming everywhere—millions of gaping mouths!" This swamp smorgasbord stars Ray Milland as a crippled, animal-hating patriarch who tries to poison every tiny life on his everglades island for a meeting of his hateful clan. But frogs organize legions of snakes, lizards, worms, insects, scorpions, alligators, and even snapping turtles to take back the island and go on from there. As another advertisement for the film reads, "Today the pond...tomorrow the world."

NO-BLOODED KILLERS

Ever since H. G. Wells' creepy, creeping, 1927 short story "The Flowering of the Strange Orchid," there have been a lot of plants out there that crave a meaty change from Ortho products. The Addams family's carnivorous pet plant had a healthy appetite but was affectionate. Unfortunately, most of the rest of the flora of horror were much less socialized.

Sometimes the plant's presence was unexplained. In *Mothra* (1962), Infant Island had a very beautiful but hungry specimen, especially when it came to Japanese scientists. The Antarctic made unwilling tree surgeons out of sailors as well as a blonde bombshell (played by Mamie Van Doren), forcing them to fight walking, acid-bleeding trees in *The Navy vs. the Night Monsters* (1966). Nonetheless, killer plants could also spring up for a couple of reasons.

They could be accidental occurrences, like the exotic hybrid, Tabanga, the tree monster in *From Hell It Came* (1957). Created when a murdered South Seas prince was buried in an atomically radiated tree, the plant looked uncannily like a stumpy cousin to the boy-gulping suburban tree in Steven Spielberg and Tobe Hooper's *Poltergeist* (1982) and the girl-grabbing apple trees in *The Wizard of Oz* (1939).

The mean greenies could also be inflicted on us from afar. Just ask the unfortunate scientist stranded in Antarctica with that hungry carrot. Janette Scott also learned more than she ever wanted to about galactic gardening as she battled mobile, poison-tentacled, giant carnivorous weeds brought by a meteor in *Day of the Triffids* (1963). And the meteoric crystals that dropped on a desert town in *The Monolith Monsters* (1957) sure grew like plants. These killer rocks not only sucked every ounce of moisture from anyone who touched them, but they also grew as tall as a skyscraper until they crashed, destroyed, and splintered—only to grow again.

Of course, chlorokill could always be cultivated. Roger Corman's *Little Shop of Horrors* (1960) boasted the not-so-delicate petal, Audrey, who actually sang for her supper and gave "Feed Me!" a whole new meaning. B movie regular George Couloris gave his darling a similar kind of fertilizer in *The Woman Eater* (1957). Back in the greenhouse, Professor Nolter's prize-winning, six-foot-six-inch (195cm) *Venus Flytrap Man in Mutations* (1974) engulfed and ingested its prey just like the real thing.

Being Replaced by Machines Is Bad Enough

The idea of a killer computer doesn't seem that far-fetched these days. But long before the information superhighway claimed its first hit-and-runs, Luddites were painting a black picture of computers. Hal the computer got his mission objective a little mixed up and started killing astronauts in *2001: A Space Odyssey*. Women were literally replaced by computers in *The Stepford Wives* (1975); who could forget that supermarket Muzak or Paula Prentiss short-circuiting from being stabbed in the kitchen? Russian and American supercomputers ended the Cold War and agreed to rule the world together in *Colossus: The Forbin Project* (1970).

Computers may not have been the villains of director Robert Wise's screen adaptation of Michael Crichton's (of *Jurassic Park* fame) *The Andromeda Strain* (1970), but they were still an

Something about that smile is just a little too placid. Patrick O'Neal dials and deals as Nanette Newman goes on automatic pilot in *The Stepford Wives* (1975).

intimidating part of the Luddite nightmare. (The story was based on real NASA concerns that returning Apollo astronauts might bring back a space plague.) Here, a returning space probe unleashes a deadly germ-warfare virus on a small New Mexico town, which kills everyone but a baby and an old drunk. The research team sent to deal with the plague must operate in a colossal, cavernous, computerized, superclean isolation center built deep below the desert floor. The hitch is that the center acts as a huge computerized body into which they have just brought toxins, and like any good immune system, it tries to expunge them. (How ironic that the six-sided soundtrack records that accompanied the movie's release destroyed countless high-tech turntables.)

Wayward computers perhaps reached their height of infamy with the world's first rapist computer in *The Demon Seed* (1977). When supercomputer Proteus' master threatens to shut it down, the machine extracts his revenge by trapping its master's wife (Julie Christie) in their house, fetishistically toying with the human object of his desires and eventually impregnating her.

ABOVE: These two scientists are wondering why this baby has been spared when almost everyone else has fallen prey to The Andromeda Strain (1970), the first of Jurassic Park author Michael Crichton's novels to be put on the screen. BELOW: Julie Christie will be more than man-handled by this ambitious automaton before The Demon Seed (1977) is over.

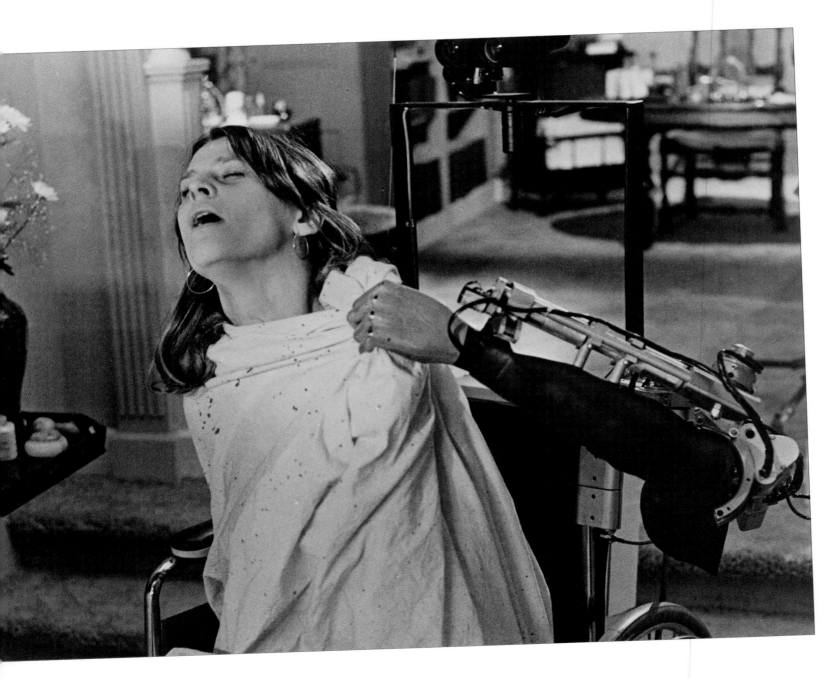

The voice of Robert Vaughn makes Proteus sound almost human. Luckily for Christie's character, the computer is humane enough to let the fertilized egg gestate in a separate incubator. The baby looks human enough once it sheds its scales. But the voice it emits in place of an infant's gurgle gives the words "I live" a distinctly metallic ring—truly the next generation in computers.

One of the strangest, if not best, killer computer movies ever made has to be the Dutch film *The Lift* (1983). Here, one character's words, "Those damn machines will be the death of us all someday," were never truer. A now-catatonic specialist in computerized elevators has installed something quite sinister in one of Rising Sun Electronix's office-building elevators. Lightning strikes the building, and the "Lift" almost bakes four inebriated diners descending from a restaurant, then opens to give a blind passenger a drop into nothingness. When one of the security guards investigates, the doors pin his head inside the shaft, and the descending elevator guillotines him. In the eeriest scene, the "Lift" plays a deadly game of peekaboo with a toddler who has been left in the lobby next to the bank of elevator doors. First one set of doors opens, then another, and another. Finally, one opens with the elevator between floors at about toddler height. The little girl probes her doll into the intriguing darkness. Crunch!

License to Kill

As reports of annual highway fatalities demonstrate, it's not all *My Mother the Car*, *The Love Bug*, and *Chitty, Chitty, Bang, Bang* out there on the freeway. Cars can be metal coffins as well as shining steeds. Sometimes they have a mind of their own. Vehicular vengeance was the theme of the television film that became Steven Spielberg's ticket into features. While putting together the pilot for *Night Gallery*, he made *Duel* (1971), a classic, terror-out-of-nowhere movie.

Dennis Weaver plays a traveling salesman who drives along the road, minding his own business, when an ugly ten-ton (9t) truck he has gotten stuck behind waves him around to pass—directly into an oncoming car. From then on, Weaver is in front of the truck, and it (or its barely seen driver) will never rest until it has destroyed the target of its fury. There is almost no dialogue in the film—and none needed. Just one man driven to the brink of death and madness by a modern machine turned prehistoric demon does all the talking necessary.

Spielberg wasn't alone in making high-octane monstrosities. While aliens could be blamed for *Killdozer*'s 1974 rampage, *The Car* (1977) sent a demonically possessed black sedan chasing a sheriff (James Brolin), his family, and anyone else that got in its way through the desert. Ironically, the car was patterned after

Spielberg's own "Jaws," and just about the same size. But the king of "re-possessed" vehicles is Stephen King, whose tales have hit and run audiences, twice.

Hell hath no fury like a red 1958 Plymouth Fury scorned. John Carpenter's *Christine* (1983) is anything but ladylike (unless the lady is a metal Medea). Rolling down the assembly line to strains of George Thorogood and the Destroyers' "Bad to the Bone," Christine opens the film by killing a factory worker who has had the nerve to leave cigarette ash on her upholstery. Her first owner also dies in the driver's seat. Twenty-one years later, she works her black magic on a high school nerd named Arnie (Keith Gordon) and metamorphoses him into a cool dude. The only problem is that Arnie starts dating, and Christine gets jealous. How do you stop a car that drives by itself just to kill people, can lock its victims inside, and can regenerate any part damaged in battle? Why, you go after it with another bigger, meaner set of wheels, of course.

Vehicles didn't get bigger or meaner than the satanic semis that rolled into King's later screen work, *Maximum Overdrive* (1986). Based on his short story "Trucks," the film depicts a doomsday scenario that pits humanity against everything with an axle, specifically those frequenting a freeway truck-stop service station. Like the Brenner family in *The Birds*, Emilio Estevez and his blue-collar cronies hole up in an island of safety surrounded by predators. And as in *The Birds*, their escape at the end doesn't signify a happy, serene future.

Face it. In the end, there's no place to run to where paws, wings, fins, antennae, microbes, microchips, and Goodyear radials can't follow (except space—and we *know* what's waiting out there). With all the victims of technology, and technology itself out for blood, we might as well roll up our sleeves, give, and give generously. Who knows—there might be just enough of the red stuff left over to start writing that apology note (to whichever species it may concern) that's been long overdue. With unnatural nature, a letter beats a visit every time.

No joy ride for this chick. She just stepped inside "the other woman," and "Christine" likes to leave her competition in the dust...or under it.

Chapter Five

THE HUMAN MONSTERS

He admitted that the rumor that he had buried a dog alive was correct, but claimed that the animal was moribund from distemper when he buried it. He denied having buried horses alive....The day of the murder she had him charged with disturbing the peace and cruelty to animals. He had carried her favorite kitten into the house writhing on the end of a pitchfork.

—Case study of sadist Fred B., from *The Mind of the Murderer,* Manfred Guttmacher, M.D., 1962

Babysitting took a nose dive and slasher films skyrocketed in popularity after John Carpenter's Halloween *hit the screen in 1978. Jamie Lee Curtis (left) braces herself for her attacker's entry, as well as an onslaught of less satisfying sequels, as escaped mental patient and killing machine Michael Meyers prepares to do what he does best.*

Here are a few of the items that Sheriff Art Schley and Captain Lloyd Schoephoerster found in the ruined Plainfield, Wisconsin, farmhouse of handyman Ed Gein on November 16, 1957: two human shinbones; two human lips on a string; two human noses on a table; ten human skulls; a soup bowl made from half a skull; ten female heads hacked off at eyebrow level; four female faces peeled off and painted with makeup; four more women's faces in plastic bags; a chair upholstered with human flesh; a vest, leggings, a purse, bracelets, and a drum made from human skin; a freezer stacked with wrapped human organs; and Gein's mother's torso on a meat hook in the barn. That cannibalistic connoisseur, Ed, became the basis for the human monsters in *Psycho* (1960), *The Texas Chainsaw Massacre* (1974), *Deranged* (1974), and *The Silence of the Lambs* (1992). Albert Einstein may have been wrong about one thing. Perhaps God does play at dice, at least genetically. Gifts, tendencies, deficits, and afflictions—a glitch or two in the DNA code is all it takes to create the great Glenn Gould or the ghoul Ed Gein.

BAD BOYS

Hollywood and a horrified public have long been fascinated by real-life victims who victimize others. "Saucy Jack," a.k.a. "Springheeled Jack," a.k.a. "Jack the Ripper" was perhaps the first mass murderer to hack his way to the silver screen. Was he a vengeful doctor? A deranged nobleman? Or was he invented as a political cover-up for the less-than-royal philanderings of Queen Victoria's grandson? No one knows. But between late August and early November 1888, in the foggy Whitechapel slums of London's East End, someone skillfully used a scalpel to eviscerate and mutilate five down-on-their-luck prostitutes.

Forty years later, another English fiend needed a hit film, and took Marie Belloc Lowndes' novel *The Lodger* as the premise for his third film. Alfred Hitchcock's 1926 silent picture of the same name tells the story of a stranger who comes to a rooming house while London is in the grip of Ripper terror. The main character was originally intended to be a sinister man who bewitches his landlady's daughter, but matinee idol Ivor Novello pressured Hitchcock to make the ending reveal that the character is an innocent man hunted; ironically, the imposed theme became one the director would return to again and again. More pressure from distributors and his producer convinced the maestro to mainstream his darkly arty film into popular suspense. Though the terror is diluted, *The Lodger* is full of atmospheric shots as well as one brilliant view of the lodger through a transparent floor as he paces in his room.

Since then, some of Hollywood's best, worst, and most popular nightmares have been based on human monsters, real and imagined, especially those who have preyed on women. Jack the Ripper himself has been reincarnated by the diverse likes of Laird Cregar, Peter O'Toole, Klaus Kinski, Jack Palance, and David Warner. *Hands of the Ripper* (1971) left Jack's daughter (Angharad Rees) to pick up her father's handiwork, and even an African-American actor has taken a turn with the scalpel in *Black the Ripper* (1975).

Of course, some monsters can be real charmers, that is, until the knife comes out. Emlyn Williams' script *Night Must Fall* (made in 1937 with Robert Montgomery and in 1964 with Albert Finney), about a Welsh lady-killer with a fear of thunderstorms, was based on Patrick Mahon, a married man who dismembered his mistress, kept her head in a hatbox, and was hanged for his sins in 1924.

Even more memorable was *Night of the Hunter* (1955). Part fairy tale, part tale of terror, part morality fable, the film marked Charles Laughton's stunning directoral film debut. Based on Davis Grubb's bestselling 1953 rural thriller, the film tells the story of switchblade-carrying, widow-marrying, psychopathic preacher and ex-con Harry Powell (Robert Mitchum), and his relentless hunt for stolen money hidden in a doll carried by one unfortunate little girl and her brave brother. Laughton and cinematographer Stanley Cortez steeped themselves in D. W. Griffith and German expressionist films in preparation for a river journey that straddled myth and reality, thanks in part to James Agee's flawless script.

The result, though a box-office bomb, was extraordinary. A corpse billows almost ethereally under river water by moonlight. The preacher's tattooed fingers (H-A-T-E is on one hand; L-O-V-E is on the other) help him deliver twisted sermons. A bridal boudoir becomes a vaulted chapel of death and sexual rage. The

ABOVE: Sir Anthony Hopkins (as Hannibal "The Cannibal" Lecter) is about to set french-kissing back a thousand years, as he gets ready for a quick bite in The Silence of the Lambs (1992). OPPOSITE: The Hitchhiker (Edwin Neal) preps Sally (Marilyn Martin) for a different kind of down-home barbecue in Tobe Hooper's nightmarish The Texas Chainsaw Massacre (1974).

What psycho-preacher Harry Powell (Robert Mitchum) doesn't want us to see us is what's waiting on the other hand. His mesmerizing performance is just one reason to see Charles Laughton's malevolently magical screen adaptation of Davis Grubb's Night of the Hunter *(1955).*

mellifluous Mitchum performs with "an icy unctuousness that gives you chills," according to *The New York Times*, and his bellow of animal rage when wading through a river to grasp at the escaping children is, in the words of writer John McCarty, "one of those isolated moments in psychofilm when the viewer can't help experiencing a cold breeze from hell run up his spine." The final moral battle for the children between the vulpine Mitchum and a rifle-toting Lilian Gish pales any armageddon pyrotechnics from many other modern movies.

Peter Kurten, a German child-murderer, was the inspiration for Fritz Lang's first talkie, originally entitled *The Murderer Among Us*. Though the film was based on Germany's famed sexual psychopath, UFA's studio chief saw the initial title as a veiled attack on his beloved Nazi party. *M*, as the film came to be known, embodied expressionism at its best. There were no ludicrously designed sets but enough visual artistry to create a nightmare world for the terrible pathos of Peter Lorre's performance as Ernest Becker, a child murderer who is finally hunted down and tried by the criminal underworld for giving them a bad reputation.

The film contains many vignettes, the sum of which makes for simple, devastating filmmaking. Becker invites a child playing with a ball to join him for some candy; the child's ball silently rolls into an empty frame in the next shot. In another scene, Becker plies another child with a shiny balloon; later in the film, we see the balloon caught in the telephone lines. The chase scene is just as remarkable, too, for Lang's cameras follow Becker into narrower and narrower confines, lending the felling of a rat in a maze, ultimately corralling him into a makeshift cellar courtroom. There, before a mob that included real criminals whom Lorre and Lang had rounded up themselves, Becker spills his guts: "The specters are always pursuing me unless I do it. And afterward, standing before a poster, I read what I have done. Have I done this? I don't know anything about it. I loathe it. I must loathe it. Must!" When asked why he made such a disturbing film, Lang's standard reply was: "to warn mothers about neglecting their children."

Another cult classic came from Michael Powell, the acclaimed director of such great films as *Black Narcissus* (1947) and *The Red Shoes* (1948). The director had originally intended to do a film on

> *After my head has been chopped off, will I still be able to hear, at least for a moment, the sound of my own blood gushing from the stump of my neck? That would be a pleasure to end all pleasures.*
>
> **—Peter Kurten to a prison psychiatrist before being guillotined**

Freud, until he heard that John Huston had beaten him to the punch. Instead, Powell made *Peeping Tom* (1959), a film about the darker side of the psychiatrist's couch.

Peeping Tom is no mild-mannered voyeur movie, as it tells the story of Mark Lewis (Carl Boehm), a handsome young focus-puller for a British film studio who dabbles in pornography on the side. Much further to the side, however, is his obsession with a documentary on fear, thanks to his father, a behavioral psychologist who made his son the human guinea pig for sadistic filmed experiments on the effect of fear on the nervous system (the film itself was actually a family affair—Powell played Mark's father, and Powell's son played the tortured younger Mark). Not only does Mark force himself to watch these "home movies," he also continues his father's work with a horrible twist. Engaging prostitutes and models in photo sessions, he films their agonies as he impales them with a blade mounted on his tripod. And as the blade is in the center of a parabolic mirror, the last thing the victims see is a hideous distortion of their own death struggle. Unfortunately, Mark isn't content with screening and masturbating to these filmed gems: he has an itch to share them with his girlfriend...and perhaps film her.

To heighten the drama, much of the movie is shown through Mark's viewfinder, making the audience the biggest voyeurs of all. Critics rushed out of the theaters and clawed over one another to denounce it. One *London Tribune* reviewer wrote: "The only really satisfactory way to dispose of *Peeping Tom* would be to shovel it up and flush it swiftly down the sewer." We beg to differ.

If only it were as innocent as mere pornography. Unfortunately, Mark Lewis (Carl Boehm) has another kind of film in mind in this scene from Michael Powell's career-destroying Peeping Tom.

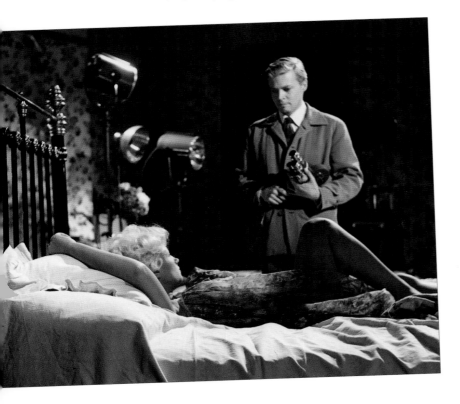

Setting the Norm(an) for Psychos to Come

> We scratch and claw but only at the air, only at each other—and for all of it we never budge an inch.
>
> —Anthony Perkins, *Psycho*

The voyeuristic eye played a big part in another film the following year. See the motel office parlor festooned with the dark eyes of dead stuffed animals...a picture from the Bible hangs on the wall, entitled *Woman Bathing Overtaken by Voyeurs*...behind the painting, a peephole...behind the peephole, a motel guest undressing for her shower. Horror writer Robert Bloch was living thirty-nine miles (62.4km) away from Plainfield, Wisconsin, when the grisly contents of Ed Gein's farmhouse spilled into the news. Mother's torso preserved in the barn? It gave him an idea for a story. What Alfred Hitchcock did with that story became the most analyzed and adulated fear film of all time, *Psycho* (1960).

Hitchcock's own dark childhood had included carrying a note from his father to the local police chief, who, after reading it, locked young Alfred in a cell for five minutes and said, "That's what we do with naughty boys." Once grown, Hitchcock chronicled a few naughty boys of his own, like Joseph Cotten's silky, widow-killing Uncle Charlie in *Shadow of a Doubt* (1943). The collegiate thrill killers in *Rope* (1948) were based on the famed Leopold and Loeb case, but Norman Bates made them look like happy campers.

Paramount tastefully declined to back *Psycho*, which left Hitchcock to bankroll the project with $800,000 of his own. The shoestring on which the film was hurriedly shot from late November to early January was long enough for the insightful Paramount execs to wrap around their own necks. Black-and-white film was used because it was cheaper and mood-producing, as was shooting on an existing television set. And since Cary Grant had gotten $450,000 plus 10 percent of *North by Northwest's* gross in 1959, teen heartthrob Anthony Perkins was paid only $40,000 to play Norman. After screening more expensive actresses such as Piper Laurie, Martha Hyer, Hope Lange, and Shirley Jones for the role of Marion Crane, Hitchcock offered the part to Janet Leigh for a mere $25,000.

A third of the way into the movie, Hitchcock shocked the world by killing off his heroine (Janet Leigh), a plan meant to throw his audiences off balance. From then on, they had no choice but to root for nice Norman covering up for his murderous mother—that is, until they found out the truth. To keep the many secrets of this secret-filled film, Hitchcock not only put out a smoke screen, saying that he was considering Judith Anderson and Helen Hayes for the role of Mrs. Bates, but also stipulated that no latecomers be admitted to the theater.

Everything regarding the film was done Hitchcock's way. Remember, this was the man who, when asked what his idea of happiness was, responded, "a clear horizon." He was also the same man who owned twenty-eight numbered sets of the same suit. As

Fay Wray may have yelled louder and longer, but no horror heroine's howl ever sent more skin crawling than Janet Leigh's scream in the fabled shower scene from Alfred Hitchcock's Psycho (1960).

Janet Leigh testified, "[Hitchcock's] camera was absolute." Hitchcock had never forgotten the hatchet jobs that editors had done on earlier films when he had too little power and too much footage, so he planned *Psycho* down to the nanosecond.

Two of the film's most meticulously planned scenes—the knifings on the stairway and in the shower—were of course carefully constructed illusions. The rapid descent of private investigator Arbogast (played by veteran stage actor Martin Balsam) after attempting to ascend to the second floor of the Bates' house began with an empty dolly shot down the stairway focused on the floor below. A bleeding Arbogast was then shown seated in a reclining chair in front of that projected image, and simply flailed his arms and bugged his eyes as the stair bottom rushed up behind him.

The psychotic maelstrom of the shower scene may be the most discussed sixty seconds in film history. The scene's seventy-eight shots required an entire week of shooting. Hitchcock built a platform to direct from above the shower (nice view, Alf). Below, Leigh provided the head and shoulders for the close-ups, while a professional model provided anything more revealing. As for that frenzied silhouette with the knife on the other side of the shower curtain, that was Tony Perkins' double. By this time, Perkins himself was back on Broadway. He was used to a certain collaborative spirit with regard to Norman, however, as Paul Jasmin, Virginia Gregg, and Jeanette Nolan had dubbed Norman's female voice prior to Perkins' departure.

The shower scene, like the sliced-up opening credits, was storyboarded by Saul Bass. Though originally accompanied by screams and running water, Bernard Hermann convinced Hitchcock to give a listen to the superbly strident, nerve-screaming score he had composed for it. Incredibly, out of all the scene's cuts (so to speak), only one showed a blade actually touching skin (a fast reverse shot of a trick knife being pulled out of an abdomen). Illusion was everywhere: a more photogenic chocolate syrup replaced blood, while stabbed casaba melons provided an additional audio touch. Hitchcock inserted the chilling sequence that led from blood swirling down the gaping shower drain to the unseeing hole of Leigh's eyes as she sprawls facedown on the bathroom floor. (A long shot in which Hitchcock's wife, Alma, noticed Leigh swallowing, had to be completely redone.) *Time* magazine grimly noted that "at close range, the camera watches every twitch, gurgle, convulsion and hemorrhage in the process by which a living human becomes a corpse."

Psycho may have been a box-office bonanza, but Hitchcock had to field all kinds of flak for his masterpiece. Ironically, the censors who enforced the Motion Picture Production Code had no problem with the shower scene, but felt that Norman's flushing the toilet during his clean-up was in bad taste. (Toilets have turned out to be hiding places in more than fifteen of Hitchcock's films.)

One critic declared the director "a barbaric sophisticate," and many panned *Psycho* in comparison to his more tasteful films, only to turn around a few years later to hail it as a classic. Hitchcock often wondered aloud how his films could go from being failures to masterpieces without ever being successes. He also replied with typical sensitivity to one man's angry note that after *Psycho*, his wife was afraid to bathe or shower. Hitchcock wrote back, "Sir, have you ever considered sending your wife to be dry-cleaned?"

> I spent eight years trying to reach him and another seven trying to keep him locked up.
>
> —Donald Pleasence, Halloween

The Gore, the Merrier

Psycho seemed to open the floodgates for homicidal maniac films, some of which have compellingly concealed most explicit bloodletting, while others repellingly congealed it with sex to form the subgenre of "splatter films," where fear is not implied but impaled (as are many of its heroines). Former college teacher and soft-core pornographer Herschell Gordon Lewis spilled the first drops of the splatter torrent. After realizing that rape and violence were the most popular features of his drive-in features, he deleted the filler and made *Blood Feast* (1963). Crammed with as much violence as one of its actresses' mouths was crammed with cranberries, raw meat, a calf's tongue, and stage blood (to simulate her tongue being torn out), the film loosely followed the Frankenstein story. Made for a mere $70,000, *Blood Feast* grossed millions and propelled its director into deeper gore with *2,000 Maniacs* (1964). In this film, a passel of blood-thirsty, good-ole-boys from Georgia rise from the dead on the centenary of Sherman's March to Atlanta, to torture northern tourists.

SOME SCREAMS MADE IT TO THE BIG SCREEN, AND SOME DIDN'T

Sometimes the truth is stranger and much more terrible than fiction. Here is only a partial listing (in order of body count) of the real monsters who inspired Psycho and all the rest. Maybe you should look a little closer at the next friendly stranger you meet. Not for the faint-hearted.

HENRY LEE LUCAS *(Henry: Portrait of a Serial Killer [1990])—According to this one-eyed, necrophilic, child-molesting, raping murderer, his killing spree with his arsonist partner, Otis Toole, lasted nearly eight years. Across the United States as many as 170 murder cases have been closed as a result of his epic confessions. His first substantiated victim was his own mother. Toole liked to barbecue their victims. Lucas claimed not to like barbecue sauce.*

ANDREI ROMANOVICH CHIKATILO— *This Soviet school teacher was a monster who would first lightly score his conscious victims with a knife blade, only to tear at their wounds with his fingers and teeth. He cut off tongue, nose, and nipple tips. He hacked away genitalia. Lastly, he stabbed their eyes, as he believed that a murderer's image is retained on his victim's retinas. Undetected for twelve years, he killed fifty-two people, many of whom were young children.*

TED BUNDY *—This clean-cut, articulate, Republican, former top Utah law student used a short crowbar he kept hidden in a fake cast on his arm to bludgeon, sexually assault, strangle, and mutilate between thirty-five to sixty young women in a rampage across a dozen states. Caught, he escaped twice to kill more. His final Florida death sentence came after suffocating a twelve-year-old in the mud as he sodomized her.*

JOHN WAYNE GACY *—This jovial, overweight, solid citizen of Illinois, who liked to babysit for friends and entertain in a clown suit, was convicted in Chicago on March 12, 1980, for killing and sexually torturing* thirty-three boys between 1972 and 1978. He convinced *many victims to allow him to show them a rope trick, looped a noose over their heads, and garrotted them. Receiving a phone call during one such strangling, he left his semiconscious victim still standing, only to resume his murder after the call. Twenty-seven bodies were found buried under Gacy's house out by O'Hare Airport. Though known to have sometimes killed two boys in one night, he said that the only crime he was guilty of was operating a cemetery without a license. He was executed in 1994.*

JEFFREY DAUMER *(The Milwaukee Cannibal)—This mild-mannered chocolate-factory worker lured seventeen young men into seclusion with the promise of pay for sex or posing for pornograpic pictures, only to drug, strangle, dismember, and eat many of them. Neighbors called the police when a frantic fourteen-year-old boy escaped drugged and bleeding at the knees, elbows, and buttocks from Daumer's apartment. Daumer convinced the officers that the boy was nineteen and that the two had had a lover's spat, then took the boy back inside to strangle him. At the time of his arrest, a human heart was found cooking on the stove of his reeking apartment. He was murdered in prison.*

CHARLES WHITMAN *(The Deadly Tower [1976])—After typing a confession on July 31, 1966, this ex-marine and University of Texas at Austin student drove to pick up his wife, dropped her off at their apartment, then proceeded to his mother's, whom he stabbed in the chest and shot in the back of the head. He then came home, wrote a few more confessional lines, and stabbed his wife to death while she slept. The next morning, he hauled a dolly full of food, water, ammunition, and firearms to the top of the twenty-seven floor campus* tower, bashing in the receptionists's skull on the way, and began randomly sniping at anyone he spotted. He killed sixteen people and wounded another thirty before being brought down by police. His former psychiatrist's notes included, "At one point (Whitman) said he was thinking about going up on the tower with a deer rifle and start shooting people." An autopsy revealed a brain tumor.

PETER SUTCLIFFE (The Yorkshire Ripper)—This frail, sensitive truck driver from northern England courted his young wife with strict propriety for seven years. He was also a self-styled Jack the Ripper who became the target of the largest criminal manhunt in British history. The murderer of thirteen women, he ritually bashed in the head of every victim with a hammer, and then frenziedly mutilated her torso with knives, screwdrivers, and even hacksaws.

ALBERT DESALVO (The Boston Strangler [1968])—Between June 1962 and March 1963 this devoted family man strangled and/or raped thirteen women, confessed to police, reneged, and was put away for earlier crimes. He sued Twentieth Century Fox for defamation over the 1968 film The Boston Strangler starring Tony Curtis. Six years after incarceration in Walpole State Prison, he was found stabbed to death in his cell. He was referred to by his lawyer, F. Lee Bailey, as "a completely uncontrolled vegetable walking around in a human body."

EDMUND EMIL KEMPER III—When this six-foot-nine-inch (205.7cm), 280-pound (127.1kg), twenty-four-year-old mama's boy with a 130 I.Q. turned himself in, he had killed, decapitated, and raped his hated fifty-two-year-old mother. He cut out her larynx and ground it up in the garbage disposal, and invited her fifty-nine-year-old best friend over for dinner, then killed and raped her as well. He obligingly led police on a meticulous search to uncover the bodies of six teenage girls he'd also slain. He was identified as the former fifteen-year old who had spent five years at a state mental hospital for shooting his grandparents to death. He claims to have memorized the results of twenty-eight different psychological tests to convince his doctors that he was fit for release.

RICHARD FRANKLIN SPECK—On the night of July 14, 1966, this itinerant seaman and garbageman broke into the living quarters of nine nurses working at Chicage Commmunity Hospital. After tying them up in a bedroom, he took them one by one into another room to strangle or stab them to death. One survivor, Corazon Amurao, hid under the bed while one of her friends was killed above her. Her glimpse of Speck's "Born to Lose" tattoo brought the killer to justice.

JOHN REGINALD HALLIDAY CHRISTIE (Ten Rillington Place [1970])—This mild-mannered, hypochondriacal, prudish, English clerk drugged, raped, strangled, and buried seven women including his wife in the charnel house of his suburban home and garden at 10 Rillington Place. He also killed a thirteen-month-old infant that belonged to one of the women and allowed her slow-witted father to be sent to the gallows for the crime. He kept a human thigh bone to prop up his garden fence and a small can filled with his victim's body hair.

DAVID BERKOWITZ (The Son of Sam)—Between July 1976 and July 1977 this pudgy postal worker, convinced that he was possessed by a six-thousand-year-old devil named Sam who barked orders at him through a neighbor's dog, shot or stabbed seventeen people (many of whom were sitting in parked cars), killing six of them. He also set 1,488 fires. The panic in New York caused five thousand people a day to call police.

RICHARD CHASE (The Sacramento Vampire)—Convinced that his blood grew thinner and his heart weaker day by day, this twenty-eight-year-old worked his way up the food chain, killing and drinking the drained blood from pets, farm animals, and finally six people before he was arrested. He also ate live birds.

The rest is B movie history and continues in Paul Leder's *I Dismember Mama* (1972), in which a serial killer falls in love with a nine-year-old girl. In *Last House on the Left* (1973), director Wes Craven reworks a Bergman script into a vengeance nightmare concerning a trio of rapists. In the Italian *Suspiria* (1976), an American dance student lands in a bloodbath at a posh European private school. In *Bloodsucking Freaks* (1976), the Grand Guignol is resurrected in Manhattan, and a dwarf tends caged, naked, cannibalistic women, one of whom gets her brain sucked out through a straw. In Merv Zarchi's *I Spit on Your Grave* (1977), Buster Keaton's grandniece plays a woman who gets to castrate a rapist with an outboard motor. You get the picture. John McCarty cuts to the heart of the matter when he says in his book on splatter movies, "[They] aim not to scare their audiences, necessarily, nor to drive them to the edge of their seats in suspense, but to mortify them with scenes of explicit gore. In splatter movies, mutilation is indeed the message—many times the only one."

Out of all the thrashing and trashing of splatter films, a few crazed killer movies managed to swim back a little toward the mainstream and even spawn a subgenre all their own that would come to be known as the teen slashers. Adolescents, illicit sex, and escaped psychopaths have made a mountain of money for horror makers of late. Standing on the top of that funereal mound of Benetton-clad hard-bodies is one dude, named simply The Shape.

When John Carpenter made the first *Halloween* in 1978, he created the most memorable psychokiller since Norman Bates. This psychokiller possessed the frenzy of a human soul in torment and the seeming immortality of a truly inhuman monster. The success of the hybrid required a mere $320,000 budget and made it back a hundred times over. *Halloween* not only left the public hungry for sequel after sequel, but with an appetite large enough to admit an imitator with a mask, a day, and sequels all his own: Jason (*Friday the 13th* [1980]).

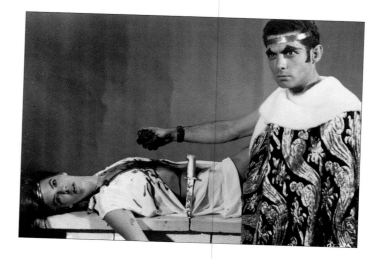

Michael Meyers (a.k.a. The Shape as played by Dick Warlock) is what his psychiatrist, Dr. Loomis (played by longtime horror veteran Donald Pleasence), refers to as "pure evil." Imprisoned in a mental institution at the age of six for fifteen years after putting on a Halloween mask and hacking up his teenage sister with a kitchen knife for the sin of having sex with her boyfriend, Michael has been silently waiting to escape from his padded cell. When he does, he returns to his small Illinois town to pick up the tools of his trade (rope, knives, and a mask) and head for the old homestead, where (surprise) three teenage girls and their dates are planning a cozy Halloween night. He takes them out one by one, the bad girls first. Last but not least in his line of victims is to be the virginal Laurie (Jamie Lee Curtis).

The movie moves unstoppably and unpredictably, its opening flashback scene recorded in one long, sinisterly smooth shot, thanks to Carpenter's Panaglide camera. Carpenter's sense of shadow and placement terrorize us, leaving no frame well lit enough to feel safe, and allowing The Shape to appear and vanish from odd corners of the screen. Carpenter toys with his hysterical audience by building attacks that don't happen and inflicting the real thing the moment things seem to relax. Even Carpenter's eerie, home-composed music is unnerving. Of course, as Dr. Loomis' bullet finally sends the seemingly indestructible bogeyman crashing out a window to his sure death, the body vanishes into the night.

Another of the most renowned just-west-of-tasteful slasher films came from former anti–Vietnam War moviemaker and Peter, Paul, and Mary documentarian Tobe Hooper. The film's title alone had audiences in a sweat before the first image flickered onto the screen. *The Texas Chainsaw Massacre* (1974) was shot on a shoestring budget in 110°F (43.3°C) Texas heat, conditions almost as inhuman as the movie itself (and conditions in which one of the director's battered actors threatened to kill him). The plot is based on three inbred, necrophiliac, cannibalistic brothers—all ex-slaughterhouse employees—and their bloodsucking, corpselike

ABOVE: Actually filmed in fabulous 'Blood-Color,' The Blood Feast (1963) was just that, as proven by the hunk of heart in this high priest's hand. OPPOSITE: Gunnar Hansen's squealing Leatherface is just one of the fiends who give chase in The Texas Chainsaw Massacre (1974).

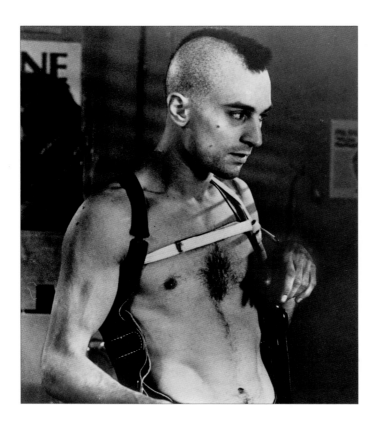

Are you talking to me? Robert De Niro (shown here as Travis Bickle) improvised some of his own dialogue in Martin Scorsese's blood-soaked psycho-saga, Taxi Driver (1976).

grandfather, who, in his prime, slaughtered sixty cattle in five minutes. All four men have become squatters on the old homestead of some unfortunate visiting teens.

While less than graphic (you only see a chain saw cut flesh once), the film's heroine, played by Marilyn Burns, gets to witness all the atrocities (she is hung on a meat hook while her boyfriend is filleted, for example) the squealing, skin-wearing, chainsaw-wielding Leatherface (Gunnar Hansen) can muster, making this one of the scariest films of all time.

The masks have come off and the stage blood orders have been reduced in the seventies, eighties, and nineties, but "man as monster" horror has continued to be vivid. Writer Truman Capote's riveting account of two drifters' brutal November 11, 1959, murder of a Kansas family and their subsequent capture and trial gave things a literary jump start in Richard Brooks' In Cold Blood (1967). Robert Blake's performance as Perry, an aspirin-chewing, guitar-playing, human time bomb, set a standard for all sympathetic but lethal psychopaths to come. Likewise, Scott Wilson as Dick Hickock, the hail- and-well-met con man who sets the bomb to ticking, is just as sweetly sinister. Shot in black and white, the film has a real documentary style, even in the fantastic scene where the duo pick up the two most vulnerable hitchhikers that ever took a ride from a couple of killers. The slow-motion effects in the film's final frames don't just chill the blood—they freeze it.

Teens got a bit of their own back in 1973 with Badlands, director Terrence Malick's wild ride that recreated the 1958 cross-country killing spree of twenty-five-year-old Charles Starkweather (dubbed the "Mad Dog Killer" by the press) and his fifteen-year-old girlfriend, Caril Ann Fugate. Under the pseudonyms Kit and Holly, Martin Sheen and Sissy Spacek give two wholesomely murderous performances on record as the couple who leave eleven dead in the wake of their teen-romance, narrated travelogue. How can you not like a killer who offers his pocket comb, pen, and lighter as souvenirs to the National Guardsmen who capture him? Who could hate a freckle-faced girl who brings her schoolbooks along on a rampage, so as not to fall behind in her studies? This is real horror manna.

The working man could be a time bomb, too. Martin Scorsese had steeped himself in blood as far back as his days at New York University's film school with his short The Shave. Showing a man shaving to that classic tune of Noxzema shave cream fame, "The Stripper," as he blithely slices his face to ribbons, could have pointed to a promising career in horror. But Scorsese chose to make movies about horror and joys he knew about: the streets of New York and the people who dwell there.

In 1976 he supercharged his own career, as well as that of a young actor named Robert De Niro, with the tale of "a nobody who dreams of being a somebody." Taxi Driver might not be a horror movie, but it's more horrifying than many films that are classified as such. As Travis Bickle, De Niro gives one of the most disturbing and dysfunctional performances in movie history. Whether he's just cruising through Times Square's scummy streets in his evil sunglasses and Mohawk haircut, wolfing sugary cereal and maple syrup in front of the television, or outfitting his personal arsenal while practicing macho lines in the mirror (many of which were improvised), he earns his place in the pantheon of screen psychopaths.

Conversely, Bob Fosse steeped his sociopathic killer in slightly loftier strata of sleaze. Crossing the continent to Los Angeles' glitzy world of soft-core pornography in Star 80 (1983), Fosse managed to create one of the least erotic movies ever made. But scary it was. Eric Roberts plays Paul Snider, the classless, fame-hungering hanger-on, who hung onto Playboy's 1979 Playmate of the Year, Dorothy Stratten (Mariel Hemingway), long enough to bring her into the big time and then get left behind. Paul didn't like getting left behind. The rest is tabloid history. There are few film scenes as creepy as Paul practicing smiles in a mirror. He might have even gotten some tips from Travis.

Dennis Hopper, who seems to have specialized in playing psychos, from the wacked-out photojournalist of Francis Ford Coppola's Apocalypse Now (1979) to the mad bomber of Speed (1994), hit an all-time high (nitrous-oxide gas mask and all) as Frank in David Lynch's supremely twisted tale of scary suburbia (and warm-up for his television series, Twin Peaks), Blue Velvet (1986). In a little town called Lumberton, Frank teaches his sex slave, Dorothy Valens (Isabella Rossellini), whose husband and son he is holding hostage, and her would-be rescuer, Jeffrey Beaumont (Kyle MacLachlan), a thing or two about madness and mayhem. Sickos don't get any sicker than Frank.

Suburbia was made almost as scary and mass murder even more folksy in 1987 by the bravura acting of Terry O'Quinn as a family man with a very bad track record in *The Stepfather*. It's a lot of pressure making your family the perfect family unit. When they let you down, it's time to start shopping for a better unit (of course, another identity is required for that) before "cutting" ties with the old. In the meantime, a basement workshop is a convenient place to let go a little. O'Quinn's alternately tongue-in-cheek and terrifying performance makes this saga of suburban slaughter very worthwhile.

Many have vied for the honor of inheriting Norman Bates' and Michael Meyers' bloody mantles. Actor Michael Rooker even got two chances to go on killing sprees: first, he starred as the doo-wop–playing murderer in the tempestuous Al Pacino–Ellen Barkin vehicle (written by Richard Price), *Sea of Love* (1989); then, he starred in the unflinchingly graphic, documentary-style account of one-eyed, necrophiliac, child-molesting rapist Henry Lee Lucas' almost mythic killing career (he was responsible for as many as 170 deaths) in *Henry: Portrait of a Serial Killer* (1990). But the real king of killers can only be Dr. Hannibal Lecter.

Thanks to novelist Thomas Harris, two actors have brilliantly incarnated this astute psychoanalyst whose taste for Mozart is only surpassed by his taste for human flesh: British thespian Brian Cox in Michael Mann's *Manhunter* (1986), and Academy Award winner Sir Anthony Hopkins in Jonathan Demme's *The Silence of the Lambs* (1992). Cox's pasty-white aesthete with a brute's face and a predator's sense of smell, and Hopkins' slick-headed, ice-eyed, nasal-voiced Tweedle Dum, are civilized supermonsters at their most lethal. Demme also managed to resurrect Ed Gein's fashion sense for the film's wily skinner, Buffalo Bill, whose sartorial taste extended to costumes made of human flesh.

> *Lizzie Borden took an axe and gave her father forty whacks. When she saw what she had done, she gave her mother forty-one.*
>
> **—child's nursery rhyme**

More recently, Glenn Close has made men think twice about extramarital activity, as the rabbit-boiling book editor of Adrian Lyne's *Fatal Attraction* (1987). Kathy Bates took home an Oscar for her portrayal of wholesome homicidal nurse Annie Wilkes, who is Paul Sheldon's (James Caan) number one fan (and number one threat to his life) in Rob Reiner's 1990 film of Stephen King's *Misery*. Jennifer Jason Leigh got to try on more than her roommate's clothes in *Single White Female* (1992), while Lara Flynn Boyle demonstrated the perverse pinnacle in employee dedication to Timothy Hutton in *The Temp* (1993). In 1994, Cult director John Waters let Kathleen Turner rival Terry O'Quinn for folksiness in the tongue-in-cheek *Serial Mom*. Even innocent little Juliette Lewis, victim to Robert De Niro's southern psycho in Scorsese's *Cape Fear* (1991), has had her moment in the bloody sun, as Mallory, one half of the deadliest couple (the other half being Woody Harrelson as

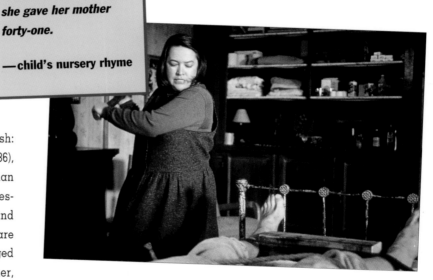

Kathy Bates shows audiences how the hand that heals can be the hand that harms as she swings back to put James Caan in more **Misery** *(1990).*

Mickey) to hit the road since Kit and Holly, in Oliver Stone's visual assault and media-mangling message, *Natural Born Killers* (1994). "Do you think I'm sexy, now?" is a question that men all over are answering just a little more carefully.

One of the best loony ladies of filmdom was also one of its most glamorous. Catherine Deneuve wasn't selling Chanel when she went to work in *Repulsion* (1965). This time, the beauty was the beast. Polish director Roman Polanski was trying to make the bridge from Europe to Hollywood when producers Michael Klinger and Tony Tenser approached him to write a speculative low-budget horror script. Polanski and his cowriter, Gerard Brach, wrote the script in seventeen days with "one overriding aim in mind: to ensure that Klinger and Tenser financed it."

Mercenary as their motives were, what Polanski and Brach created is one of the most disturbing psychological horror films ever. The story line depicts the psychotic break of Carol, a beautiful

BAD GIRLS

Psycho's shower victim Marion Crane got her revenge: women would get the chance to do a little filleting of their own on film. Jean Arless got to play both parts of a *Homicidal* (1961) married couple looking to cut the competition out of a family inheritance. In *Strait-Jacket* (1964), an ex–axe murderess, played by Joan Crawford, passed on some traits to her daughter that would have done Lizzie proud. Jessica Walters got to intimidate the hell out of late night deejay Clint Eastwood, as the crazed groupie in his *Play Misty for Me* (1971). Margot Kidder doubled as homicidal separated Siamese twins in Brian De Palma's sick thriller of horror on Staten Island, *Sisters* (1972), and Ruth Roman took a slice at playing Jill the Ripper in *A Knife for the Ladies* (1973). In 1982, Rita Mae Brown's script of *Slumber Party Massacre* even allowed girls to avenge themselves on a power drill–wielding psycho with a power saw.

and sexually repressed French manicurist, as seen through her own eyes, hallucinations and all. When left alone in her sister's apartment for a long weekend, Carol crumbles as madness begins to set in. At first, the paranoia is as subtle as cracking sounds in plaster, but soon, big hairy arms are reaching through those cracks, and eventually rapists break down her bedroom walls. Unfortunately, Carol gets real visitors that weekend as well. The results are unpleasant.

Deneuve hardly says a word during the film, but she sells every second of torment. Polanski had based her character on a former acquaintance whose "air of sweet innocence and demure serenity" belied the fact that "she was simultaneously attracted and repelled by sex as well as prone to unpredictable bouts of violence." He also played on the lack of awareness that often blunts the perceptions of those who live with the disturbed; the family photograph in the film's final frames tells all on that count.

BAD SEEDS

There's nothing quite as terrifying as the innocent made malevolent—and who are more innocent than children? Ray Bradbury tapped into the fear of evil kids in the forties with his short story "The Small Assassin." Bradbury turned postpartum depression into a parent's nightmare, thanks to a newborn whose nightly crawls included positioning toys strategically on the stairs and snuffing the gas pilot in his parents' bedroom. In "The Veldt," Bradbury gave readers apple-cheeked, wide-eyed youngsters who had lions attack their parents when deprived of the virtual reality machine in their playroom. William Golding took a tribe of British schoolboys, crashed their plane on a tropical island, and watched them degenerate into murderous savages in his famous novel *Lord of the Flies* (which hit the screen in 1963, thanks to British directing innovator Peter Brook).

Of course, it wasn't long before Hollywood was investigating little monsters. William March's 1954 novel, *The Bad Seed*, asserted that heredity is responsible for criminal behavior. Director Mervyn LeRoy brought the theory to the screen in the 1956 film of the same name, with Patty McCormack as the towheaded nine-year-old killer, Rhonda Penmark. Rhonda is an impatient girl. When an elderly neighbor promises her a trinket in her will, Rhonda pushes her down the stairs to hasten the bequest. When a schoolmate gets the penmanship medal she feels she deserved, she drowns him at the school picnic. When a handyman suspects her as the murderer, she traps him in a burning shed. When her mother discovers the monster she's been protecting, she poisons both Rhonda and herself—but Rhonda survives! Because Section 12 of the Production Code wouldn't permit children to be incited to commit crimes, LeRoy tacked on a new ending to the film: Rhonda gets struck by lightning while fishing out her penmanship medal from the creek where her mother had thrown it.

Rhonda set a precedent for little blond monsters. *Village of the Damned* (1960) was full of them. Based on John Benyon Harris' (*Day of the Triffids*) science-fiction thriller *The Midwich Cuckoos*, the film took a sleepy little English hamlet and rendered its inhabitants unconscious for several hours while some alien force impregnated every childbearing female. The resulting twelve platinum-blond offspring grow with abnormal speed to become cold-hearted telepaths possessing incredible power, and adults are soon involuntarily killing themselves in rather hideous ways. The kids here are truly creepy, and designer Eric Aylott's blond wigs that make their little foreheads bulge don't make them look one tiny bit nicer.

Here is one damsel best left in distress. Beauty has never been more beastly than Catherine Deneuve's comely psychotic in Roman Polanski's Repulsion *(1965).*

Another deadly bevy of blond babes came courtesy of one of John Carpenter's favorite horror filmmakers. David Cronenberg's *The Brood* (1979) cemented the Canadian director's reputation for both repelling and fascinating audiences. Here, the terror target was obstetrics. (By 1988, Cronenberg would have made his way to a related field with the truly terrifying tale of demented, drug-addicted, twin gynecologists [played by Jeremy Irons] in *Dead Ringers*.) Imagine getting so angry that your rage manifested itself as horrible little demons spawned from fleshy sacks inside your thighs. Well, that's what happens to Nola Corveth (Samantha Eggar) at the Somafree Institute of Psychoplasmatics under the care of Dr. Hal Raglan (Oliver Reed). These demons look like a clutch of snowsuited killer kiddies, and they savage anyone resented by the insane Nola. Eventually, the Brood turns its

> *As James lay dying, Robert Thompson picked him up. Careful to avoid getting blood on his clothes (because, he said later, "blood stains, doesn't it, and then my mother would have to pay more money"), he laid the child face down across one of the rails. Living near the railway as he did, Thompson knew the times of the trains, and perhaps thought the death could be made to look like an accident. A large number of bricks were piled on James's head and upper torso, almost like a shrine.*
>
> —The final moments of two-year-old James Bulger's life. Lured from a Liverpool shopping mall, dehumanized with paint, beaten, pummeled with bricks, and knocked unconscious with a twenty-two-pound (9.9kg) metal plate, his jaw was torn open and stuffed with garbage by ten-year-olds Robert Thompson and Jon Venables. From "Children of Circumstance" by Blake Morrison, *The New Yorker*, February 14, 1994

Look into their innocent eyes for too long and you might slit your throat, just like the grown-ups in Village of the Damned *(1960)*. The film was remade by John Carpenter in 1995.

> To me, the mind/body split is the source of the mystery, and also the horror, which I think we ultimately have to confront. You see people whose minds are perfectly together while their bodies begin to distort, begin to change, begin to age, begin to rot, whatever: that, to me, is horror.
>
> —David Cronenberg

attention to Nola's ex-husband and their adorable normal sister, Candy (Cindy Hinds). Cronenberg, who was involved in a custody battle of his own while making *The Brood*, affectionately calls the film his "Kramer vs. Kramer."

Sometimes the mutations actually were infants: Larry Cohen (creator of television's *The Invaders*) tested the parental bond with his fanged, mutant, milkman-killing baby in *It's Alive* (1974) and *It Lives Again* (1978). Sometimes they were older: the precocious Tuesday Weld took turns wickedly wielding pliers, a gun, and her adolescent sexuality while manipulating Anthony Perkins in *Pretty Poison* (1968). The next year unleashed a matricidal and patricidal teenage brother and sister on an unsuspecting Shelley Winters in *The Mad Room*. In 1972, the pen of Thomas Tryon, former alien from *I Married a Monster from Outer Space*, let loose twisted twin boys on a touching scene of Americana in *The Other*. As recently as 1992, former *E. T.* innocent Drew Barrymore tried out a few Lolitaesque moves of her own in *Poison Ivy*.

Most recently, the littlest villain has been everybody's favorite good boy. Macaulay Culkin (*Home Alone*, 1990) reveled in his badness as the sociopathic Henry in the 1993 production of Ian McKewan's *The Good Son*. What would be music to the ears of a

kid who is capable of drowning his little brother, impaling dogs with a crossbow, dropping dummies onto the interstate at rush hour, and throwing his little sister through the ice of a frozen pond? "Hi, my mom just died and I have to stay with you while my dad's away on business." Culkin's cousin, Mark, comes to stay with him and soon learns the truth behind the renowned Culkin grin, thus dedicating himself to preventing future family accidents. The decision Henry's mom is faced with by the movie's climax makes *Sophie's Choice* seem like a quiz show question.

So, the next time you're about to dole out a little discipline, think twice before that palm meets bottom. You might want to do a quick frisk first. Kids are growing up awfully fast these days, and one of the things they're learning faster than any other generation before them (thanks to politicians and television) is how to deceive and how to kill. With stories of gun-toting ten-year-old gang members, and privileged children slaughtering parents as standard fare on the news, "diminutive adults" might be a better label for some of our little ones. For though ten-year-olds Robert Thompson and Jon Venables picked up two-year-old James Bulger in a Liverpool shopping mall and lured him to a stretch of railroad tracks, where they tortured him to death, they later claimed that Chucky from *Child's Play* (1988) had made them do it. Human monsters come in all sizes.

Bad Vibes

Science tells us that most people only tap into the tip of the cranial iceberg. Death-predicting psychics, heckled spoon-benders, number-obsessed idiot savants, crucified prophets, earless painters, palsied mediums, and other exceptions to that rule don't always enjoy their special gifts, which can seem more like special curses. And as with most people with brains that are developed way behind their emotional maturity and control, getting angry can be a messy business. Here's a parade of potent paranormals that moviedom has made into legend. See if you can match up the movie, the star, and that special ability.

Sissy Spacek in Carrie (1976).

Movie	Star	Ability
1. BLINK	A. Drew Barrymore	a. Sexually charged shaman with skill akin to the martial art of kung fu
2. CARRIE	B. Alan Bates	b. Can unleash living horrors from personal nightmares
3. THE DEAD ZONE	C. Faye Dunaway*	c. Musician with newly restored sight can see a murderer whom nobody else can see
4. DREAMSCAPE	D. Michael Ironside	d. A real mover and shaker on prom night
5. THE EYES OF LAURA MARS	E. Zelijko Ivanek	e. Pyrokineticist
6. FIRESTARTER	F. Sissy Spacek	f. Photographer focuses through the eyes of a killer
7. THE FURY	G. Andrew Stevens	g. Can make someone's head swell until it explodes
8. SCANNERS	H. Madeleine Stowe	h. Can tell a lot about people's futures just by holding hands with them
9. THE SENDER	I. Dennis Quaid	i. Can make John Cassavetes cry big red tears
10. THE SHOUT	J. Christopher Walken	j. Can rid you of nightmares by getting inside them

* The film was originally intended to star Barbra Streisand, who ended up only singing the theme song.

Answers
1=H,c; 2=F,d; 3=J,h; 4=I,j; 5=C,f; 6=A,e; 7=G,i; 8=D,g; 9=E,b; 10=B,a

Chapter Six

DARK ROADS
ARE BETTER
LEFT UNTRAVELED

The woods are lovely, dark and deep,
But I have promises to keep,
And miles to go before I sleep,
And miles to go before I sleep.

—Robert Frost, "Stopping by Woods on a Snowy Evening," 1923

Practice dying.

—Plato's last words

Famous friends? Marvelous mothers? Easy to work with? Never! Nevertheless, these two temperamental titans (Bette Davis and Joan Crawford) weren't afraid to get down and dirty in one of the sickest sister acts Hollywood ever filmed, Whatever Happened to Baby Jane? (1962).

Hamlet tried to warn us. There are more things in heaven and on earth than are dreamed of in most of our philosophies. Just ask the flock at Jonestown or in Waco; just ask the next of kin to the satanic sacrifices of Richard "The Night Stalker" Ramirez; just ask anyone who has had to sell his or her house because of nocturnal activities that can't be explained; just ask the fat cats now wandering the streets in soiled business suits after one snort too many; just ask audiences.

When the lights come up in the theater and the Saturday-afternoon-creature-feature-martian-invasion-teen-screamer is over and our adrenaline has dropped, life goes on. If, in addition, metaphysically and psychologically terrifying issues have flowed from the screen to be absorbed by our consciousnesses, lingering to prey on core beliefs and fears, that creeping flesh creeps right out of the theater with us.

Restrained believability in horror is often horror at its best and most terrifying. Stories that seriously deal with mist-shrouded questions of mind, mortality, and spirit haunt us in a way that Dracula, The Thing, and The Shape only wish they could. Contemporary writers such as Clive Barker (*Cabal, Night Breed, The Great and Secret Show, The Hellbound Heart, Imajica, Clive Barker's Books of Blood*), Stephen King (*The*

> **The dead have highways.**
>
> **They run, unerring lines of ghost-trains, of dream carriages, across the wasteland behind our lives, bearing an endless traffic of departed souls. Their thrum and throb can be heard in the broken places of the world, through cracks made by acts of cruelty, violence and depravity. Their freight, the wandering dead, can be glimpsed when the heart is close to bursting, and sights that should be hidden come plainly into view.**
>
> **—Clive Barker, *Clive Barker's Books of Blood*, 1986**

Shining, The Stand, Cujo, Carrie, Christine, Pet Sematary, The Dark Half, Needful Things, Gerald's Game, It), Ramsey Campbell (*The Count of Eleven, The Face That Must Die, The Hungry Moon, Night of the Claw, Parasite, Incarnate, Demons by Daylight*), Peter Straub (*Ghost Story, Koko, Mystery, Shadowland, Floating Dragon, Julia, If You Could See Me Now*), and Ian McKewan (*The Cement Garden; The Comfort of Strangers; First Love, Last Rites; The Innocent*) have proved this so, not by purging the demons from the dark, but by opening readers' minds to let the bad guys in. From time to time, Hollywood has caught on to that concept.

SOMETIMES THEY COME BACK

What happens when we shuffle off this mortal coil? Do we go to heaven? Hell? Are we reincarnated? Oblivious? Is our energy converted to an astral plane? Do we walk toward the brightest light imaginable? And what happens to those who are killed so suddenly, unhappily, or violently that they don't know that they are dead? Do they hang around? If they do, what do they want with us?

Constance Bennett and Cary Grant may have stayed to entertain their old friend, Cosmo, in *Topper* (1937), and Jennifer Jones may have posed sweetly for a lonely artist after drowning in a storm off Cape Cod in *Portrait of Jennie* (1948). Patrick Swayze may have wafted in from the beyond for one last kiss with Demi Moore in *Ghost* (1990), and Bill Cosby might have been the perfect *Ghost Dad* (1990). Alan Rickman may have compassionately come back (complete with an intergenerational, international men's club of the departed) to trick his wife (Juliette Stevenson) into giving up the ghost in *Truly, Madly, Deeply* (1992). But these are the exceptions: all spirits are not blithe out there.

For some poor souls, reincarnation isn't even a possibility. Herk Harvey's amazingly everyday but amazingly creepy black-and-white mood piece (shot exclusively in Lawrence, Kansas) *Carnival of Souls* (1962) plunges church organist Mary Henry (Candace Hilligoss) off a bridge into a river during a Sunday drive with her girlfriends. Hours after sinking, Mary drags herself out alone. Shaken, she moves to a fresh start in another town, but things start to go very wrong, and Mary begins to lose her mind.

Dead faces beckon to her from mirrors and windows. On the outskirts of town, an abandoned lakeside pavilion, where hundreds were drowned, inexplicably pulls her to prowl it. She has fits where the sound drains out of her world and people seem unaware of her presence. Only the final frames tell us why she is drawn so torturously away from the living.

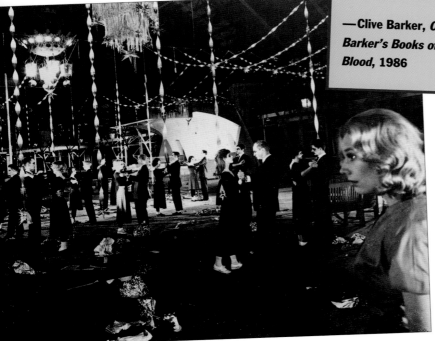

Candace Hilligoss is asking herself where all the corpse-white dancers came from and why she's so sickly drawn to an abandoned pavilion in the sinister black-and-white sleeper **Carnival of Souls** *(1962).*

A maternal Mia Farrow examines the child's toy that will become the instrument of her undoing in **The Haunting of Julia (1977).**

Ghosts have more often come back with malevolence. Director Jack Clayton learned that ghost-loving author Henry James had become a fan of Freud's after writing *The Turn of the Screw* in 1895. Clayton hired American novelist Truman Capote and British playwright John Mortimer to adapt William Archibald's stage play of James' work for the screen, but with a psychosexual bent. The result was the eerily ambiguous *The Innocents* (1961). A prim repressed governess, Miss Giddens (Deborah Kerr), takes a position at a remote estate, only to become convinced that her young charges were somehow involved in the sadistic relationship between their now-deceased former governess, Miss Jessel, and their valet, Quint, and may now be possessed by them.

Thanks to cinematographer Freddie Francis (who would become Hammer Film's mainstay in years to come) every baroque image is filled with sexual malevolence, though nothing is overt. A glistening bug crawls between the lips of a fallen cupid statue. The boy's goodnight kiss seems strangely adult. Miss Giddens' music box picks up the melancholy dirge the boy sings. The spinster gets so worked up that she sees shapes lingering in the shadows.

What's called for? An exorcist for all, a caseworker for the kids, or a hot date for Miss Giddens? The horrific end leaves the unsettling question hovering in the Gothic air—so unresolvedly, in fact, that Marlon Brando was induced to incarnate Quint himself in *The Nightcomers* ten years later.

Peter Straub's stories have also inspired Hollywood filmmakers. Two movies based on his work have brought she-spirits in for the kill with a vengeance, *Ghost Story* (1981) and the far superior *The Haunting of Julia* (1977). *The Haunting of Julia* tells the story of a young malevolent spirit. It seems that Julia (Mia Farrow) has accidentally been involved in the death of her own young daughter and now pays the price of self-

EXCUSE ME, IS THAT BLOOD ON YOUR ARMANI?

Don't let them fool you. Many stars climbed a gore-covered rung or two while ascending the ladder to mainstream fame.

Name	Horror Film
Jason Alexander	THE BURNING
James Arness	THE THING
Raymond Burr	GODZILLA
Marilyn Chambers	RABID
Bruce Dern	HUSH...HUSH, SWEET CHARLOTTE
Clint Eastwood	TARANTULA
Arlene Francis	MURDERS IN THE RUE MORGUE
Larry Hagman	BEWARE! THE BLOB
David Hedison	THE FLY
Margot Kidder	BLOOD SISTERS
Nastassja Kinski	TO THE DEVIL—A DAUGHTER
Werner Klemperer	DARK INTRUDER
Michael Landon	I WAS A TEENAGE WEREWOLF
John Laroquette	THE TEXAS CHAINSAW MASSACRE
Steve McQueen	THE BLOB
Sal Mineo	WHO KILLED TEDDY BEAR?
Jack Nicholson	THE TERROR
Oliver Reed	CURSE OF THE WEREWOLF
Ralph Richardson	THE GHOUL
Dean Stockwell	THE WEREWOLF OF WASHINGTON
John Travolta	CARRIE
Pia Zadora	SANTA CLAUS CONQUERS THE MARTIANS

EXCUSE ME,
IS THAT A DIAMOND ON YOUR CLAW?

What doesn't happen on the way up can happen on the way down. When the calls stop coming and the rent is due, what's a former star to do? Here are the horrors that awaited these former heroes and heroines in the September of their years.

Name	Claim to Fame	Maim of Shame
Fred Astaire	Top hatter	GHOST STORY
Joseph Cotten	Citizen Kane's pal	LADY FRANKENSTEIN
Joan Crawford	Mommie Dearest	I SAW WHAT YOU DID
Bette Davis	What a dump!	THE NANNY
Kirk Douglas	Spartacus	THE FURY
Henry Fonda	Tom Joade	THE SWARM
Joan Fontaine	Rebecca's successor	THE DEVIL'S OWN
Zsa Zsa Gabor	Green Acres star	PICTURE MOMMY DEAD
Ava Gardner	Ole Blue Eyes' ex	TAM LIN
Gloria Grahame	It's a Wonderful Life's *bad girl, Violet Bick*	BLOOD AND LACE
Alan Hale	Skipper on Gilligan's Island	GIANT SPIDER INVASION
Laurence Harvey	The Manchurian Candidate	TENDER FLESH
Howard Keel	Showboat *songman*	DAY OF THE TRIFFIDS
Burt Lancaster	Wyatt Earp	THE ISLAND OF DOCTOR MOREAU
Elizabeth Montgomery	Bewitched's *Samantha*	THE LEGEND OF LIZZIE BORDEN
Agnes Moorehead	Samantha's mom	DEAR DEAD DELILAH
Debbie Reynolds	Singing in the rain	WHAT'S THE MATTER WITH HELEN?
Henny Youngman	Violin-playing top banana	GORE GORE GIRLS

recrimination and loneliness. In her misery, she moves out on her husband (Keir Dullea) and into a new house to escape the memories, but finds her maternal instincts rekindled by visitations from an unhappy little spirit. The stuff of happy endings, were it not that the ghost child is not her babe at all, but the spirit of a frilly young sadist who once cast a spell over tots to kill some other children. This doesn't stop guilt-ridden Mia from saying, "Come to mama!" The final tableau of mother and child is enough to freeze the blood.

It seems that the most compelling reason any ghost ever came back is hunger—the kind of hunger found only in *Night of the Living Dead* (1968). With music borrowed from fifties science-fiction films, an African-American hero (Duane Jones), black-and-white stock film, and an initial budget consisting of $600 collected from nine other filmmakers (he received another $100,000 down the road), Pittsburgh's George Romero created a monster movie that changed the face of horror forever. The film was shot in thirty days over a seven-month period.

Robert Englund's creation, Freddy Krueger, may be the longest-lived (and most popular) villain to ever stalk the scream screen. Notice the manicure as he grabs yet another teenager in A Nightmare on Elm Street 4 (1989).

The plot is simple. A Venusian space probe brings back a molecular mutation, which causes anyone recently deceased to rise mindlessly from the earth with one motivating purpose: to eat human flesh. The horror is nonstop, for from almost the beginning of the film, frantic humans have holed up in an abandoned house to fend off the hungry zombies.

Night of the Living Dead stunned audiences by showing flesh-eating in the flesh, complete with sounds of slurping, tearing, and gnawing, and plenty of entrails (thanks to an investor who was a butcher) to look at. One of the most horrifying scenes shows a little girl contentedly feeding on the arm of her father, whom she has just killed. Film critic Roger Ebert was so nauseated that he used the film as an example of how Hollywood horror corrupts (an interesting comment from the man who wrote *Beyond the Valley of the Dolls*) and, in doing so, brought the sleeper to critics' attention.

Finally, one supremely malevolent and popular ghost deserves recognition. He's given the word *manicure* a whole new meaning. Returned child-killer and dream nemesis Freddy Krueger (Robert Englund) burst upon the scene in 1984 with direc-

GROSS-OUT KING GEORGE ROMERO SPILLS GUTS ON SAVINI SPECIAL EFFECTS FOR DAY OF THE DEAD

[Tom] Savini and crew did the effect [cutting open a zombie on the operating table] using a table with a lowered "pit" section cut into the middle. When the person playing the zombie [Mick Trcic] got on the table, his chest and torso would sink onto a platform below the pit, while his head and legs remained up on the level surface. The resulting "dip" where his chest and torso would be if he were lying flat was built back with a false, hollow "chest cavity" made of foam latex, which was glued into place on his real chest. The chest cavity was painted black inside to give it the illusion of depth and was then filled with a variety of animal entrails...chunks of foam latex "flesh." Trcic simply turned over to spill the guts onto the floor.

—From *The Zombies That Ate Pittsburgh: The Films of George A. Romero*, by Paul Gagne, 1987.

tor Wes Craven's visionary *A Nightmare on Elm Street*. Craven, a former fundamentalist Baptist (who didn't allow himself the pleasure of seeing a film until college) and humanities professor with advanced degrees from Johns Hopkins University, was inspired to make a movie by two articles he had read. The first article was a 1979 newspaper clipping concerning young men who were having such awful dreams that they denied themselves sleep, only to fall asleep anyway and dream they were dying from their nightmares. The second article discussed the rumor that the Russians were doing experiments in both dream manipulation as well as assassination through psychic intervention.

Believing that new ground lay in "hallucinatory horror not restricted to day-to-day reality," Craven made a different kind of teen screamer. Freddy Krueger is the vicious, omnipotent bogeyman who had been burned to death by the irate parents of the children he had killed only to make his return into the dreams of four high school pals (including Edward Scissorhands himself, Johnny Depp)—with fatal results.

The deaths in this film are as grisly and as gut-wrenching as horror gets. The first dreamer who Freddy visits gets shoved up a wall and sliced to ribbons by unseen hands. The girl's boyfriend's bed sheets snake around his neck as he lies in a jail cell and drag him up the bars to hang him. The third friend is sucked down into his own bed; then gallons upon gallons of blood erupt out of it and fountain up to the ceiling. The lone survivor, Nancy Thompson (Heather Langenkamp) wages a one-woman battle to stay awake, and finally to bring the razor-fingered fiend out of her dreams to kill him again.

A Nightmare on Elm Street risked an "X" rating several times along the way, but two weeks after its limited opening, it had grossed two million dollars, and less than a year after its release, Freddy was riding as Grand Marshall of the Greenwich Village Halloween Parade. Though sequels have been plentiful, the talking Freddy Krueger doll got pulled from the toy shelves because it scared children.

FREDDY'S LITTLE HELPERS

Wes Craven did not direct by vision alone. He had the expert help of special effects wizard Jim Doyle and makeup miracle worker David Miller. Here's how the trio engineered some of the 104 effects in the first of the A Nightmare on Elm Street series—and some of the most memorable effects in horror history. (By the way, those hands building Freddy's gloves in the opening credits are Doyle's.)

Freddy always sports the scars of his incineration, but is never above a few techno-embellishments as shown here in A Nightmare on Elm Street 3 (1987).

What You See	What You Don't See
Freddy bulges through the wall at the head of Tina's bed	**Doyle stands behind a painted sheet of spandex**
A force makes Tina crawl up the wall and across the ceiling	**Doyle's revolving room, which can be tilted at any angle**
Freddy's twelve-foot (3.6m) arms	**They're inflatable**
A hand comes up between Nancy's legs as she bathes	**Heather is actually sitting on a submerged Doyle at the top of a 450-gallon (1.703.2 l) tank. (What started out as a two-hour shot expanded to a waterlogged twelve)**
Rod is strangled in his jail cell	**A complex series of piano wires and cables manipulate the sheet**
Nancy runs up quicksand stairs	**The stairs are coated with Bisquick and chopped carpet**
Tina tries to scream in her dream but coughs up dust	**The dust is pulverized Captain Crunch cereal**
Fiery footsteps up the stairs and a flaming Freddy throttling Nancy's mom (Ronee Blakly)	**Pyro gel and stuntman Tony Cecere, who specializes in being set on fire**
Freddy's sparking finger-knives	**A wall is rigged with a wire mesh that runs twenty-four volts of juice into Robert Englund's grounded gloves**
Freddy's fabulous face	**Miller preferred translucent white skin that reveals muscles underneath, but Craven preferred the pussed-up, stripped-down look. Englund spent 1½ hours every day donning twelve nonreusable foam latex pieces. Twenty-five sets were made in all**
Slashes are made by an unseen hand on Tina's torso	**A model is cast of Amanda Wyss' body, into which slits are made and blood inserted. Monofilament lines open the covered slits, allowing blood to flow. There were no nipples on the dummy, as nipples and slashes equal an "X" rating**
Freddy opens his own chest	**A torso is cast. Jim Picciolo—a professional maggot wrangler—lends a hand**
Mom's final exit into the house	**An inflatable dummy wearing a Ronee Blakly mask is yanked with a cable through a small window in the front door**
Terrified teens are whisked away in a possessed car	**A true moment of fear caught on film. The device slamming the convertible's roof down did so with such excessive force that the teen actors inside were truly terrified**

FOR GOD'S SAKE, GET OUT!!!

What would unrestful spirits be without a place to be unrestful in? Haunted houses have been a horror staple since Walpole's Castle of Otranto. Like their Victorian and Gothic predecessors, early films often contained secret passages and sinister butlers, such as James Whale's collaboration with Boris Karloff, *The Old Dark House* (1932). But only later did these films take tongue from cheek long enough to give any real goose bumps.

Many believe *The Uninvited* (1944) to be Hollywood's first serious go at bringing haunted houses to the screen. In this film, atmosphere is the watchword. Ray Milland and Ruth Hussey star as a brother and sister who buy a big old house high on a cliff on the coast of Cornwall. There, the two become entangled with the troubled daughter of the former owner. It seems that two ghosts, one protective and the other menacing, are haunting the girl, driving her to literally jump off a cliff. Romance and horror hold hands under the table, for Victor Young's theme song, "Stella by Starlight," wafts as ethereally as the scent of mimosa (the good ghost), or the sound of muffled sobbing (the evil ghost) in the night.

Serious haunting wasn't really hazarded again in Tinseltown until almost twenty years later, when director Robert Wise adapted Shirley Jackson's story *The Haunting of Hill House*. Like humorous horror showman William Castle's *House on Haunted Hill* (1958), *The Haunting* (1963) concerns outsiders who dare to take up residence in a haunted house to do supernatural research.

Wise, who went on to direct *The Sound of Music* two years later, focused on the presence of the twisted old house and its subtle interplay with the possibly twisted minds of its occupants (Julie Harris plays a neurotically repressed virgin, with paranormal experiences; Claire Bloom, a lesbian psychic; Richard Johnson, an obsessed anthropologist; and Russ Tamblyn, a cynic). Subtlety reigns, yet there is nothing delicate about the merciless pounding on the front door (almost bowing it to splinters) at the film's climax.

The sixties and seventies brought a number of well-known houses to the screen. Roger Corman borrowed from H. P. Lovecraft's "The Case of Charles Dexter Ward" in *The Haunted Palace* (1963), a film that featured Vincent Price in one of his most restrained and scary performances as a regular guy who returns to his ancestral New England home, where he becomes possessed by the spirit of his burned-at-the-stake warlock great-great-grandfather, whose curses have populated the small town with horrible mutants and put something incredibly nasty down the family well over the generations.

> Hill House, not sane, stood by itself against its hills, holding darkness within; it had stood so for eighty years.... whatever walked there, walked alone.
>
> **—Shirley Jackson, The Haunting of Hill House, 1959**

Increasingly, ghosts discarded rattling chains and billowing curtains for slightly more explicit and provocative maneuvers. That same year, Corman also gave Francis Coppola (there was no Ford in his name back then) his first directing break with a skillful, axe-swinging, *Psycho*–clone set in an Irish castle: *Dementia 13*. Director John Hough was also able to do something sexually explicit in *The Legend of Hell House* (1973): have a medium commune with a spirit in a distinctly carnal way. (Barbara Hershey would take this un[super]natural act to new heights of violence at the hands of an ectoplasmic rapist in *Entity* [1983].) In *The Amityville Horror* (1979), a highly embellished but true story of the Lutz family's twenty-eight-day nightmare at the hands of a colonial house that had been the recent scene of "parenticide," Margot Kidder got to put down the cutlery and clutch her mortgage. Plagues of flies and goo-vomiting plumbing may have taken some of the subtlety out of the haunting, but they certainly increased box-office shock value.

Julie Harris is caught between attraction and repulsion as she gets closer to an encounter with the supernatural in the supremely psychological ghost tale The Haunting *(1963).*

Robbie (Oliver Robbins) tries to save his little sister, Carole Anne (Heather O'Rourke), from getting sucked through her bedroom closet into another dimension in Tobe Hooper and Steven Spielberg's collaboration, Poltergeist (1982).

Haunted houses reached hallucinatory heights of horror in the eighties, with two films that weren't really about houses at all. Pity the poor families of Cuesta Verde Estates, whose suburban dream homes have been built over a bulldozed graveyard. There goes the neighborhood. *Poltergeist* (1982) brought together the unlikely pairing of producer Steven Spielberg and director Tobe Hooper to make a simultaneously playful and menacing family odyssey.

From *Poltergeist*'s star-spangled opening credits, you can tell that the Freelings (Jobeth Williams and Craig T. Nelson) are regular thirty-something, pot-smoking parents of the eighties. You ignore obvious warning signals like a parakeet burial, animated car toys tripping delivery men, and ghost movie references because everything is just too chaotically, suburbanly normal—that is, until their ten-year-old daughter (Heather O'Rourke—watch out for those blond kids) starts getting messages from "the people who live inside the television set." Then things do a lot more than go bump in the night, and the real chaos begins. The poltergeist is here, and it can do lots of tricks from driving the dog to canine neurosis to playing records and flipping book pages as

the objects swirl around a room, from animating a toothy, long-armed clown to strangle its owner to destroying the whole neighborhood. By the time the horror ride is over, parapsychologists, a guilty real estate developer, a midget psychic, and even Satan himself have all dropped in for a visit. Yet all the events are unbelievably believable.

Tony Todd did a little developmental haunting of his own at Chicago's Cabrini Green projects as the hook-handed ghost of a persecuted, educated slave in Clive Barker's *Candyman* (1992): the urban landscape got "gutted" in a whole new way. But the blood spilt in the inner city couldn't come close to the carnage at Colorado's Overlook Hotel.

What should you expect from a film whose trailer shows lobby elevator doors opening to let loose a tidal wave of type A toward the audience? Expect the liberties that director Stanley Kubrick and screenwriter Diane Johnson took with Stephen King's *The Shining* (1980). They took out the topiary animals that stalk their victims in the snow and replaced them with a vast hedge maze perfect for a human minotaur. They pulled the focus from psychic son Danny Torrance (Danny Lloyd) and shifted it to deranged dad Jack (Jack Nicholson), who treads between campiness and madness, and turns in a landmark psycho performance as a caretaker who gets more than cabin fever as he cares for an evil resort high in the Rockies.

Few steady-cams ever did better work than the one that glided along behind Danny's tricycle as it prowled the Overlook's labyrinthine hallways, or the one that glided behind Jack as he chased Danny through the hedge maze. Obsessively, Kubrick took takes for individual scenes into the double and even triple digits to attain a cold, visual perfection. And nothing could be colder than the sight of the film's final image: an Overlook fandango, photographed circa 1921, with Jack smack in the middle of it.

HELL'S DOMINION

Evil, ultimate evil. Not "The Shape." Not whiny, demon-possessed serial killers. But the genuine article. As Mick Jagger can tell you, Lucifer's been around long enough to "steal many a man's soul and seal his fate." Goethe's Faust made a bargain with him. Oscar Wilde's Dorian Gray got his portrait painted with him. Stephen Vincent Benét's Daniel Webster out-talked him. Major League Baseball teams have been sold to him. Prisons, desserts, and hors d'oeuvres have been named after him. Mark Twain found his correspondence. Musicians swear he wears a blue dress. He's even had some X-rated rest and relaxation with a certain "Miss Jones."

The Devil is at his scariest in the movies. As early as 1900, he has been frolicking in films under various pseudonyms, including Emil Jennings, Ray Milland, Walter Huston, Ralph Richardson, Claude Rains, Ernest Borgnine, Donald Pleasence, Cedric Hardwicke, Burgess Meredith, Ray Walston, Rex Ingram, Peter Cook, Robert De Niro, George Burns, and Jack Nicholson.

The Devil's followers have earned a certain reputation, too. With contemporary satanists indulging in human sacrifices, it's hard to ignore their fright potential. Since the 1934 Universal pairing of Karloff and Lugosi in *The Black Cat*, a film loosely based on a real-life satanist, Alistair Crowley, Beelzebub has meant big box-office bucks.

In the early days, less seemed to be more in the brimstone department, and although one of the earliest examinations of the cult of evil—the Swedish silent *Haxan* (1921)—combined documentary lectures on medieval witchcraft with simulations of black masses, nude orgies, and sacrifices, most films were much more restrained.

> ...somewhere in sands of the desert
> A shape with lion body and the head of a man,
> A gaze blank and pitiless as the sun,
> Is moving its slow thighs, while all about it
> Reel shadows of the indignant desert birds.
> The darkness drops again; but now I know
> That twenty centuries of stony sleep
> Were vexed to nightmare by a rocking cradle,
> And what rough beast, its hour come round at last,
> Slouches towards Bethlehem to be born?
>
> —W. B. Yeats, "The Second Coming," 1920

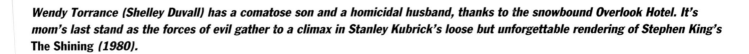

Wendy Torrance (Shelley Duvall) has a comatose son and a homicidal husband, thanks to the snowbound Overlook Hotel. It's mom's last stand as the forces of evil gather to a climax in Stanley Kubrick's loose but unforgettable rendering of Stephen King's **The Shining** *(1980).*

Strange as it may
sound, I tried not to
make a film about
Satan.

—William Friedkin,
director of *The Exorcist*

Though their names are legion, only a few metaphysical films have been frightening enough to send an unbeliever rushing to midnight mass. The all-time champion is *The Exorcist* (1973). The film's day-after-Christmas opening had audiences everywhere lined around the block to get in, and some of them fainted and vomited when they got out. Critics ranted and raved (*The New York Times* called the film "a chunk of elegant, occultist claptrap"). A priest in Chicago, for example, built his Sunday sermon upon the film, and boosted attendance: his church had to turn hundreds of gawkers away. Not since *Frankenstein* had a horror movie made this kind of splash. One of the top grossers ever, *The Exorcist* convinced Tinseltown that horror could be classy entertainment and that religion was fertile ground for fear.

Based on William Peter Blatty's novel of a young priest's test of faith (which director William Friedkin maintains was his main focus) by the Devil in possession of a prepubescent girl, the film is terrifying for a number of reasons.

The music sets it all up. Mike Oldfield's now-famous "Tubular Bells" tinkle a new-age precedent that horror films ever after have repeated. The very expensive sequence of Father Merrin (Max Von Sydow) on an archaeological dig in Iraq opens a historic can of worms. The desert scenes are full of sinister foreshadowing imagery: black and white dogs fighting, whirling dust, one-eyed beggars, stopped clocks, unexplained buzzing, vicious-looking winged statues, and nitroglycerin pills to keep Father Merrin's heart pumping against the Beast.

Jumping to Halloween in Washington, D.C., doesn't make things much better. Neither do images of a grotesquely sacrileged Virgin Mary at a local church. Neither do menacing noises coming from the attic. Little Linda Blair as Regan MacNeil doesn't help, either. She's every mother's nightmare: a sweet, horse-loving kid who's about to go completely out of control. She'll do nasty things on the living room rug in front of party guests. She'll send people greetings from their dead relatives. She'll win gold medals for her long-distance bodily functions. She'll perfect moves that would terrify any contortionist or osteopath. She'll make murderous modifications in her house's thermostat. She'll make her bedroom window a popular new exit to the house. She'll do things with a crucifix that will send the Christian world to its knees.

Still, other people besides Linda Blair can be blamed for creating such cinematic terror. Friedkin is mostly to blame for building such unendurable dread and tension before the full-blown possession takes place. It's almost a relief when it does. But it isn't, really. Then the Devil speaks. It seems Friedkin was in possession

(so to speak) of an actual tape of the exorcism of a fourteen-year-old boy in Rome. The boy's voice grew distinctly deeper and coarser under Satan's influence. Friedkin needed a voice of deep power that would be sexually unidentifiable. To get it, he went to veteran actress (and former demon in her own right in Nicholas Ray's *Johnny Guitar* [1954]) Mercedes McCambridge, who provided the gravel for so many of Regan's lovely lines, and it was a voice she would have to take considerable legal action to get credit for.

Last and far from least, we can blame the dean of Hollywood horror makeup, Dick Smith, and his soon-to-be-famous protégé, Rick Baker. No optical effects were used. Even the levitation was done live with magnetic fields (according to Friedkin). Smith's transformation of fresh-faced girl to boil-covered, blood-eyed demon is phenomenal, even to the point of raising welts that spell something on the poor kid's stomach.

Running a close second in the impetus for midnight mass attendance is Richard Donner's spin-off from the Bible's Book of Revelations, *The Omen* (1976). The film was first released exclusively to Sunday preview audiences. Gregory Peck starred as a diplomat with the stickiest family situation around since Abraham took his son for a little sacrificial stroll. When his baby (with wife Lee Remick) dies at birth, a helpful priest offers to substitute a foundling child to prevent his wife's nervous collapse.

Damien turns out to be the Antichrist himself. Biblical bloodshed permeates the plot as people around the boy meet gruesome

(John Cassavetes), move into The Dakota, a big old New York apartment building on Seventy-second Street and Central Park West. Rosemary's eccentric new neighbors are very friendly, but she is beginning to suspect that their cozy group is a coven.

Throughout the film, horror insinuates itself in insidious yet physical ways. (Cassavetes called the film "the most violent non-violent movie" he'd ever seen.) Rosemary wakes one morning after lovemaking to find long, bestial scratches on her back; she stumbles upon a recent acquaintance—who has committed suicide by throwing herself out the window of the Dakota; she dreams of being mobbed and forced to the ground by her neighbors.

Farrow became so stressed and bruised during filming that a close-up of Ralph Bellamy administering her a shot is in reality a hired nurse (wearing Bellamy's lab coat) giving her a vitamin B-12 injection. And where was the diabolical director when not filming and inflicting all this torment? Polanski, elated to be filming in the United States, home of the Western, had aquired a six-gun and holster and spent many of his off moments practicing his quickdraw.

Though contemporary vehicles for cults, devils, and demons, such as Clive Barker's film *Hellraiser* (1987), have a certain visceral impact, others appeal on a number of levels. You may have to replay the plot a couple of times in your head to come up with the big "OHMYGOSH!" but once you do, Alan Parker's stylistically slick *Angel Heart* (1987) will chill you to the bone. Along the way to the film's terrifying revelation, Parker puts private eye Harry Angel (played with distinctive disheveledness by Mickey Rourke) on a manhunt to Louisiana that quickly becomes a descent into the world of devil worship. With Robert De Niro as his evil employer, legendary bluesman Brownie McGhee as his guide, and Bill Cosby's own Lisa Bonet as the object of his desires (watch for a certain scene with dripping chicken blood that had to be altered to turn the MPAA "X" into an "R" rating), Rourke is in good company as he goes straight to hell.

Another shining example is *Jacob's Ladder* (1990). As the film's poster states, "The most frightening thing about Jacob Singer's nightmare is that he isn't dreaming." Based on the notion that the biblical Jacob dreamed of a ladder bearing earthly and angelic traffic between heaven and earth, the film features Jake Singer (Tim Robbins), a divorced husband, bereaved parent, former theologian, troubled Vietnam vet, and affable postman, who is living through a nightmare. Something happened in-country that turned his whole unit into crazed killers. He barely survived. Now home, his world is just as dark and disorienting.

The subways seem populated with demons. Jake's psychiatrist has vanished without a trace of ever having existed. His war buddies are holding a horrible secret. He's being stalked as he begins to uncover a government conspiracy. He burns with a fever that should kill a horse. Even his girlfriend (Elizabeth Peña) is

ends, including decapitation by flying plateglass and impalement by a lightning rod. Meanwhile, Gregory Peck gropes closer to the dark truth (facing demon Dobermans and the shocking remains of Damien's real mother) and learns what he must do (something having to do with seven sacred daggers). The film comes to quite a climax, with Jerry Goldsmith's menacing musical score underlining the tension. Needless to say, the cavalry doesn't exactly arrive on time. Two more sequels take Damien through his wonder years and into adulthood.

As hard as raising the son of Satan is, it's even harder when you know you're about to give birth to him. *Rosemary's Baby* (1968) brought an eclectic team together to tap into the occult fascination and God-questioning of the Aquarian sixties. Directed by Roman Polanski in his American debut and produced by showman William Castle, who was so excited by the potential of Ira Levin's 1967 novel that he bought the film rights to it three weeks prior to its publication, the film boasts a bevy of odd friends and neighbors, including Ralph Bellamy, Charles Grodin, Ruth Gordon (who won an Oscar for her work), and Victoria Vetri (*Playboy*'s Miss September 1967), the voice of Tony Curtis, and even Castle himself, in a silent, phonebooth cameo. As in Lewton's *The Seventh Victim*, half the chill is the seeming normality. (How horribly ironic it is, too, that after chronicling a cult, Polanski's own wife [Sharon Tate] would be slaughtered by one a mere two years later.)

In the film, docile Rosemary (Mia Farrow, sporting a $5,000 Vidal Sassoon coif) and her down-on-his-luck actor husband, Nick

turning into a corrupting jezebel before his eyes. As hell seems to leak into his earthly life, only his angelic chiropractor (Danny Aiello) and beckoning visions of his deceased son, Gabriel (a young Macaulay Culkin), offer him any hope. Is he losing his mind? Is he the victim of a heinous chemical conspiracy? Or is he engaged in a struggle much stranger and much deeper than he can imagine? These questions all get answered in this fine film's fine revelatory moments.

It's more than a little ironic that a film which grossed more than $70,000 in its first three days at the box office languished for seven years as a hot but untouchable property in Hollywood. Its author, Bruce Joel Rubin, who also penned the immensely popular *Ghost* (1990), was no stranger to metaphysics. After graduating from New York University Film School with classmates Brian DePalma and Martin Scorsese, he spent two years traveling through Iran, Turkey, Afghanistan, Nepal, Malaysia, Thailand, and Japan. By the time he arrived in Hollywood, he had the script in tow that was largely based on the *Tibetan Book of the Dead*—hardly typical film fare. Moguls marveled at its eloquence and excitement, but no one wanted to touch it.

"I can imagine why it went unmade for so long," confesses its eventual director, Adrian Lynn (*Fatal Attraction*, 1987), "It was incredibly intimidating. I spent a year just working on a way to film it." Lynn stumbled upon this script during the Writer's Guild strike of 1988 and immediately canceled his commitment to direct Tom Wolfe's *Bonfire of the Vanities* (1990). He spent the next twelve months looking for financial backers, watching Vietnam documentaries, reading about near-death experiences, visiting special effects houses, and hounding Rubin to tone down the apocalyptic script into something that was practical to film. The result was a rewrite that had Dustin Hoffman, Al Pacino, Richard Gere, Julia Roberts, Andie MacDowell, Demi Moore, and Madonna wrangling for the leading roles, and a movie that does the unthinkable: ask its audience to think while they watch.

***Things get a little too hot for Jake Singer (Tim Robbins) to handle in* Jacob's Ladder (1990).**

WHAT'S HAPPENING TO ME?

Some of the most effective horror movies ever made keep audiences and protagonists guessing as to what's real and what isn't...can't possibly be...but oh my God, maybe it is.

A French film (that inspired William Castle to go into horror as he and his wife saw the ticket line wind around the block) that proves the point is Henri-Georges Clouzot's *Les Diaboliques* (1955). Murder is not as simple as it seems here, as a wife (Vera Clouzot, wife of Henri-Georges) and mistress (Simone Signoret) conspire to do away with a swinish boys' school principal (Charles Vanel). They kill him and dump him in a nearby lake, but you just can't keep a bad man down. A chain of events that suggests that he is alive seem to bring both women to the brink of insanity. But then again, one of this killer twosome has been there all along—but which one?

Relative insanity and twisted endings resurfaced in a twisted tale of Hollywood itself, Robert Aldrich's 1962 film of Henry Farrell's novel *Whatever Happened to Baby Jane?* Relegated to be shot on television sets, budgeted so slimly that its two aging divas settled for a percentage of the gross (and were they glad they did!), this "baby" was anything but innocent.

A bedraggled Bette Davis tackled one of the riskiest roles a fading star ever grabbed to rise and shine with. She plays Jane Hudson, a former child star à la Shirley Temple who now lives in creepy seclusion with her invalid former-movie-star sister, Blanche (Joan Crawford). It is suggested that Blanche's career ended after an auto accident (that Jane may have arranged). Now she's a captive of her loony little sister.

Jane wears ghoulish white makeup, tries to renew her career (performing "I've Written a Letter to Daddy" while accompanied by a sleazy twenty-four-year-old Victor Buono in his first screen role), and otherwise prepares for a comeback that must have been coached by Norma Desmond (Gloria Swanson) from *Sunset Boulevard* (1950). As Jane is forced to confront the truth about her nowhere career, old hatred rises for her crippled sibling (not hard for Davis to do, as she and Crawford hated each other). A campaign of cruelty and terror begins, including dinners of dead parakeet and rat under glass.

But beneath the torture, what's the whole story? Who's the real monster? There's a horrifying human secret that we don't know. And we don't find it out until the two misfits come out of the dark to collide with the real world in a beach scene that is not reminiscent of Gidget.

> True!—nervous—very, very dreadfully nervous I had been and am; but why will you say that I am mad? The disease had sharpened my senses—not destroyed—not dulled them.
>
> —Edgar Allan Poe, "The Tell-Tale Heart," 1843

Two of psycho-metaphysical horror's most ambiguous, ambitious, and haunting works end with tragedy that is as tangible and real as a knife blade. Yet the journey to the deadly destination could be the work of madness or the hand of fate.

In Roman Polanski's Kafkaesque nightmare, *The Tenant* (1976), Trelkovsky (played with pathos by Polanski himself), a struggling Polish file clerk, rents a Paris apartment whose former tenant, Simone Choule, has just swan-dived from her window. Why? Trelkovsky visits the dying woman in the hospital. Encased in a body cast with one hole for her eye and one for her mouth, she takes one look at him and screams without stopping. Why? Trelkovsky soon suspects that the building's other tenants (which include Melvyn Douglas and Shelley Winters) had something to do with her tragedy and, what's more, have now set their beady sights on him. Why?

The film is a paean to paranoia and alienation. Polanski is masterful as both director and star, and his roaming camera on a Louma crane glides everywhere it shouldn't. Strange figures stand deathly still for hours at night as they watch Trelkovsky's dark apartment from the toilets across the courtyard. The local café owner seems intent on forcing him to adopt the suicidal woman's brand of cigarettes and cocoa. Things only get worse and more weird. Finally, he is driven to become the late Simone herself. Why? Madness? Evil? Something unsuspected? The last frame may tell you, if you can bear it.

Finally, horror can be, strange as it sounds, incredibly beautiful. Blood, fine art, family values, an exotic locale, fantastic sex, clairvoyance, serial murder, and destiny: they're all there in Nicolas Roeg's *Don't Look Now* (1973), an adaptation of the Daphne du Maurier novel. Art historian Donald Sutherland is squinting at slides of a Venetian church, which he will soon restore, when a blotch of red fills the frame. Simultaneously, his red-raincoated little daughter has wandered into the pond in their backyard. Roeg's lingering shot of this father grieving as he wades out of the water with a lifeless body in his arms is almost too personal to watch.

As Sutherland and his wife (Julie Christie) experience the kind of pain and isolation that only bereaved parents know, they go to Venice to work and forget. However, once there, forgetting death can be forgotten. A Jack the Ripper–type murderer has been making the rounds. Bodies are being fished out of the canals. The couple also bump into two elderly English sisters, one of whom, though blind, is gifted with second sight of the dead child. You can practically smell the lavender wafting from the matronly duo, who are so cool and composed that there is just a trace of malignant gloating to their silences. Are they benign biddies or crones from a coven? Sutherland scoffs, but bit by bit, Christie's grief draws her to the sinister spinsters. No sooner has she swallowed their occult line than her husband starts having both horrifying experiences and visions.

Roeg's deft editing (he began his career as a cinematographer on films such as *Fahrenheit 451* and *Far from the Madding Crowd*), Anthony Richmond's rich photography, Giovanni Soccol's lush art direction, and Pino D'Onnagio's music weave around the emotionally charged performances of the film's two stars to create something as ephemeral as it is irrevocable. The classically scored scene of Sutherland and Christie making love, intercut with their dressing and leaving and with images from their past, shows aloneness and togetherness at its most human. And the final moments pull all the pieces together with a power that is phenomenal.

As they have for so many other victims in horror's history, Sutherland's eyes have been opened by terror. Ghosts are not as gentle as he thought. The hand of fate has not led him to peace. Perhaps he was insane after all. It's a heavy price to pay for insight. But as Edgar Allan Poe's self-defense murderer in "The Tell-Tale Heart" might have told him as he was being carried away in his straitjacket, "Just because you're paranoid, doesn't mean that they're not out to get you."

NAME THAT SCREAM

Who knows what fresh horrors await films of the future? But we can always savor the past. Below are a gaggle of tell-tale lines from some of horror's high points—distant and recent. See if you can match the quote with the movie.

Quote

1. They're coming to get you, Barbara! (Done in an imitation of Boris Karloff)

2. You were always the caretaker here.

3. I never drink—eh—wine.

4. I am not Simone Choule!

5. If I let go of you now, do you think you could fly?

6. Ah, little lad. You're starin' at my fingers.

7. One of us...one of us...gooble, garble...one of us!

8. We all go a little mad sometimes.

9. It's alive! It's alive! Oh, it's alive!

10. Tell the world to watch the skies. Keep watching the skies.

11. A man-made race upon the face of the earth...why not? Our dream is only half realized!

12. A census taker once tried to test me. I ate his liver with some fava beans and a nice Chianti.

13. In this world you're a nothing, Alex, and me...I'm God.

14. Three-four, better lock your door. Five-six, grab your crucifix. Seven-eight, gonna stay up late. Nine-ten, never sleep again.

15. Looks like a good day to die.

16. Are you telling me I should send my child to a witch doctor?

17. I used to hate the water. I can't imagine why.

18. You've just blown home entertainment as we know it clear out of the water.

19. Aren't you afraid of me, you ancient hellhound?

20. It's a drug that's made from a flower that grows in India. It draws color from anything it touches.

21. I'm becoming something that never existed before. I'm becoming Brundlefly.

22. They're here.

23. Free! Free at last! Ah! Mad, eh, Lanyon? You hypocrites, deniers of life, if you could see me now, what would you think?

24. My wife sick. She wrong. That not my wife.

25. You should have been with us. There was lots of blood.

26. Good dog!

27. Abracadabra, we're dead.

28. Beat 'em or burn 'em. They go up pretty easy. They're dead, they're all messed up....kill the brain and you kill the ghoul.

Movie

A: FRANKENSTEIN

B: THE THING

C: THE TENANT

D: A NIGHTMARE ON ELM STREET

E: THE SILENCE OF THE LAMBS

F: NIGHT OF THE LIVING DEAD

G: FREAKS

H: DRACULA

I: DREAMSCAPE

J: THE SHINING

K: PSYCHO

L: FLATLINERS

M: THE RAVEN

N: CUJO

O: LORD OF THE FLIES

P: THE OTHER

Q: DR. JEKYLL AND MR. HYDE

R: THE EXORCIST

S: JAWS

T: THE GOOD SON

U: THE INVISIBLE MAN

V: NIGHT OF THE HUNTER

W: THE FLY

X: THE BRIDE OF FRANKENSTEIN

Y: INVASION OF THE BODY SNATCHERS

Z: MAGIC

AA: POLTERGEIST

BB: BRAINSTORM

Answers

1=F, 2=J, 3=H, 4=C, 5=T, 6=V, 7=G, 8=K, 9=A, 10=B, 11=X, 12=E, 13=I, 14=D, 15=L, 16=R, 17=S, 18=BB, 19=M, 20=U, 21=W, 22=AA, 23=Q, 24=Y, 25=O, 26=N, 27=Z, 28=P

BIBLIOGRAPHY

Allison, Alexander W., Herbert Barrows, Caesar R. Blake, Arthur J. Carr, Arthur M. Eastman, and Hubert M. English, Jr., eds. *The Norton Anthology of Poetry*. Rev. ed. New York: W. W. Norton and Company, 1975.

Barker, Clive. *Clive Barker's Books of Blood*. Vol. 1. New York: Berkley Publishing Group, 1986.

Beck, Calvin Thomas. *Heroes of the Horrors*. New York: Collier Books, 1975.

Brosnan, John. *The Horror People*. New York: St. Martin's Press, 1976.

Cohen, Daniel. *Horror Movies*. New York: Gallery Books, 1984.
_____. *Masters of Horror*. New York: Clarion Books, 1984.

Cooper, Jeffrey. *The Nightmare on Elm Street Companion*. New York: St. Martin's Press, 1987.

Deutelbaum, Marshall, and Leland Poague, eds. *A Hitchcock Reader*. Ames, Iowa: Iowa State University Press, 1986.

Dillard, R. H. W. *Horror Films*. New York: Monarch Press, 1976.

Ebert, Roger. *Roger Ebert's Home Video Companion*. New York: Andrews and McMeel, 1989.

Gagne, Paul. *The Zombies That Ate Pittsburgh: The Films of George A. Romero*. New York: Dodd, Mead and Co., 1987.

Guttmacher, Manfred. *The Mind of the Murderer*. New York: Grove Press, 1962.

Halliwell, Leslie. *Halliwell's Film Guide*. 8th ed. New York: Avon Books, 1978.

Hersey, John. *Hiroshima*, 1946. Reprint: New York: Knopf, 1985.

Jackson, Shirley. *The Haunting of Hill House*. New York: Viking Penguin, 1984.

Kendrick, Walter. *The Thrill of Fear: 250 Years of Scary Entertainment*. New York: Grove/Weidenfeld, 1991.

Keylin, Arlene, and Christine Bent, eds. *The New York Times at the Movies*. New York: Arno Press, 1979.

Klausner, Lawrence D. *Son of Sam*. New York: McGraw-Hill, 1981.

Lindsay, Cynthia. *Dear Boris: The Life and Times of William Henry Pratt*. New York: Knopf, 1975.

Loban, Lelia. "If Looks Could Kill." *Scarlet Street*, June 1994.

Manchel, Frank. *Terrors of the Screen*. Englewood Cliffs, N. J.: Prentice Hall, 1970.

McCarty, John. *Psychos: 80 Years of Mad Movies, Maniacs, and Murderous Deeds*. New York: St. Martin's Press, 1986.
_____. *The Official Splatter Movie Guide*. New York: St. Martin's Press, 1992.

McNally, Raymond T., and Radu Florescu. *In Search of Dracula*. Greenwich, Conn.: The New York Graphic Society, 1972.

Meyers, Richard. *The World of Fantasy Films*. New York: A. S. Barnes and Co., 1980.

Michaud, Stephen G., and Hugh Ayensworth. *Ted Bundy: Conversations with a Killer*. New York: Signet Books, 1989.

Mitchell, Robert, and Linda Mitchell. "Feed Me! (Venus Flytraps; How Things Work)." *Life*, April 1994.

Morrison, Blake. "Children of Circumstance." *The New Yorker*, February 14, 1994.

Nash, Jay Robert. *Murder America*. New York: Simon & Schuster, 1980.

Nichols, Peter. *The World of Fantastic Films: An Illustrated Survey*. New York: Dodd, Mead and Co., 1984.

Peary, Danny. *Cult Movies*. New York: Delacorte Press, 1981.

Poe, Edgar Allan. *Tales of Mystery*. New York: Puffin Books, 1990.

Pohl, Frederik K., and Frederik K. Pohl IV. *Science Fiction Studies in Film*. New York: Ace Books, 1981.

Ressler, Robert K., and Tom Shachtman. *Whoever Fights Monsters*. New York: St. Martin's Press, 1992.

Riley, Philip J., and George Turner, eds. *Dracula: The Original Shooting Script*. Universal Filmscripts Series, vol. 13. Absecon, N. J.: Magicimage Filmbooks, 1990.

Rumbelow, Donald. *Jack the Ripper: The Complete Casebook*. Chicago: Contemporary Books, 1988.

Russo, John. *Scare Tactics*. New York: Dell Books, 1992.

Spotto, Donald. *The Dark Side of Genius: The Life of Alfred Hitchcock*. Boston: Little, Brown and Co., 1983.

Stacy, Jan, and Ryder Syversten. *The Great Book of Movie Monsters*. Chicago: Contemporary Books, 1983.

Taylor, Al, and Sue Roy. *Making a Monster*. New York: Crown Publishers, 1980.

Time-Life Books. *True Crime: Compulsion to Kill*. Alexandria, Va. Time-Life Books, 1993.

Truffaut, François. *Hitchcock/Truffaut*. New York: Simon and Schuster, 1984.

Water, Stanley. *Dark Visions*. New York: Avon Books, 1992.

Weaver, Tom. *Science Fiction Stars and Horror Heroes*. Jefferson, N. C.: McFarland and Company, 1991.

Weldon, Michael. *The Psychotronic Encyclopedia of Film*. New York: Ballantine Books, 1983.

Wells, H. G. *The War of the Worlds*. New York: Ace Books, 1988.

Wilkinson, Alec. "Conversations with a Killer." *The New Yorker*, April 18, 1994.

Wright, Gene. *Horror Shows*. New York: Facts on File, 1986.

PHOTOGRAPHY CREDITS

Photographs Courtesy The Kobal Collection

Archive Photos: 108-109
Photofest: 111, 117

Acknowledgements

AIP: 57, 86 bottom; **Allied Artists:** 69; **Anglo Amalgamated:** 96; **Castle Rock Entertainment:** 103; **Cinerama:** 80 bottom; **Columbia:** 5, 48–49, 63 both, 64 top, 68 top, 87, 89, 102; **Compton-Tekli/Royal:** 104; **Delca Films:** 14–15; **Deutsche Bioscop GMBH, Berlin:** 13 top; **Embassy:** 111; **EMI:** 66; **Falcon International:** 90, 91; **First National:** 50; **Friedman-Lewis:** 100; **Goldwyn:** 18; **Gaumont/British:** 41 left; **Gouverneur Morris/Goldwyn:** 19 bottom; **Herts Lion:** 110; **Melies:** 12; **MGM:** 2, 17, 20 bottom, 22, 30–31, 36, 41 right, 80 top, 88 bottom, 106, 116; **MGM British:** 115; **Nero:** 27; **New Line:** 6, 113, 114; **Orion Pictures Corporation:** 92; **Paramount:** 8, 16, 19 top, 26, 40, 59, 97, 120; **Prana-Film GMBH, Berlin:** 15 right; **Projektions-AG "Union", Berlin:** 13 bottom; **RKO:** 39 bottom, 42, 43, 44 both, 45, 51, 52, 67, 73; **Transworld:** 54-55; **Tri Star/Carolco:** 68 bottom, 121; **Twentieth Century Fox:** 60 left, 71, 119; **United Artists:** 46, 94-95, 107; **Universal:** 10-11, 20 top, 21, 23, 24-25, 29, 30 top, 32, 37, 38, 39 top, 47, 58, 60-61, 74-75, 77 both, 78-79, 81, 84 both, 85, 88 top; **Universal-International:** 53, 55 right; **Vortex-Henkel-Hooper/Bryanston:** 93, 101; **Warner Bros.:** 62, 64 bottom, 86 top, 108-109, 117, 118

INDEX